NICK BOLLETTIERI'S

Mental Efficiency Program for Playing Great Tennis

Nick Bollettieri and Dr. Charles A. Maher
Foreword by Mary Carillo

CONTEMPORARY BOOKS
A TRIBUNE NEW MEDIA/EDUCATION COMPANY

Library of Congress Cataloging-in-Publication Data

Bollettieri, Nick.
    [Mental efficiency program]
    Nick Bollettieri's mental efficiency program for playing great
tennis / Nick Bollettieri and Charles A. Maher.
        p.   cm.
    Originally published: The mental efficiency program. 1st ed.
Cleveland, Ohio : International Merchandising Corp., 1994.
    Includes biographical references and index.
    ISBN 0-8092-3282-0
    1. Tennis—Psychological aspects.   I. Maher, Charles A., 1944–
. II. Title.
GV979.P75B65   1996
796.342'01'9—dc20   95-43600
                                                               CIP

The authors and publisher have used their best efforts in preparing this
book. The authors and publisher make no warranty of any kind, express
or implied, with regard to the instructions and suggestions contained in
this book.

Cover design by Amy Nathan

Published by Contemporary Books, Inc.
Two Prudential Plaza, Chicago, Illinois 60601-6790
Manufactured in the United States of America
International Standard Book Number: 0-8092-3282-0
10   9   8   7   6   5   4   3   2   1

TABLE OF CONTENTS

LIST OF TABLES

ABOUT THE AUTHORS

NICK BOLLETTIERI

Nick Bollettieri is regarded as one of the very best tennis coaches and instructors in the history of the game of tennis. The Nick Bollettieri Tennis Academy is the largest and most sophisticated tennis training facility with over 20 locations throughout the U.S. and worldwide. His students include Andre Agassi, Jim Courier, Monica Seles, Jimmy Arias, and David Wheaton—to name but a few—and thousands of junior and collegiate champions. Bollettieri is currently the coach of Boris Becker and Mary Pierce, as well as several of the world's top junior prospects. His career—soon to enter its fifth decade—is marked by several unique achievements: voted the World's Best Tennis Coach (1988), recipient of the Sharpshooter Professional Coach of the Year award (1989, 1990), Special Advisor on junior tennis to the USTA, and USPTA Pro of the Year (1991). In conjunction with the late Arthur Ashe, Bollettieri also initiated the Ashe/Bollettieri Cities Program providing tennis, education, and programming to inner city youth in America. A proud father of five, Bollettieri is an avid skier and body surfer when not on the court at his Academy in Bradenton, Florida, or coaching on the road.

ABOUT THE AUTHORS

CHARLES A. MAHER

Dr. Charles A. Maher has been involved with the performance enhancement of individuals, groups, and organizations for many years. He is Professor of Psychology, Graduate School of Applied Psychology, Rutgers University, where he teaches and supervises doctoral psychology students and conducts applied research. He is a licensed practicing psychologist, as well as sport psychologist to the Nick Bollettieri Tennis Academy (NBTA) and to the Chicago White Sox. Dr. Maher is internationally recognized for his work in executive achievement, sport psychology, management training, total quality management, team development, program planning and evaluation. His clients include General Motors, Ford, Nabisco, General Electric, National Aeronautics and Space Administration, Martin Marietta, and the United States Department of Education, and departments of education, labor, and human services in 38 states, Canada, the United Kingdom, Israel, and the Ukraine. Dr. Maher has authored over 300 articles in scientific and professional journals and 16 books. He holds a diplomate from the American Board of Administrative Psychology and is a Fellow of the American Psychological Association, the American Association of Applied and Preventive Psychology, and the American Psychological Society.

ACKNOWLEDGMENTS

We are pleased to acknowledge and thank various people, all of whom were influential and instrumental in the creation, development, and publication of this book.

Our foremost words of appreciation go to Bill Rompf, who has been a positive driving force since the inception of this project as well as an expert editor and technical advisor.

Relatedly, Ted Meekma's effective leadership during all stages of the book's production and publication is very much appreciated.

Tracy Wildey has been exceptional as a production and layout artist on this book.

Likewise, Claudia Cuddy has performed at peak levels providing fine editorial commentary, production skills, substantive advisement, and highly reliable work.

Furthermore, Judy Harch is to be commended for her painstakingly precise manuscript review work.

Special thanks to Jose Lambert and Martha Cobo, who have been actively involved in the design, implementation, and evaluation of the Mental Efficiency Program at the NBTA, on court.

Much thanks to Nick's good friend, Gene Winger, for his professional advice and input during the final stages of the book.

The photographs in this book were taken by James

"Jimmy Boy" Bollettieri, Nick's son, who is a professional photographer and tennis instructor. He has captured his father and his father's achievements on film for the past 20 years. We appreciate his photo contributions to this book.

In addition, we thank the many fine tennis professionals and students at the NBTA and elsewhere who have provided us with current and relevant feedback on their tennis development, who have kept us honest with tough questions and practical perspectives, and who have helped us learn about mental efficiency and positive self-development for tennis, sport, and life.

FOREWORD

by Mary Carillo, Tennis Commentator

As early as I can remember, I loved athletics, sports, games of any kind. If there was an activity that required running, throwing, hitting, kicking, or keeping score, I was right there in the thick of it all, and everything came naturally to me. That's why it was such a shock and unpleasant surprise when I first tried tennis and found it so hard. I didn't know how to grip the racket, strike the ball cleanly, defend the court, work a point, or win a match. Only because I was so unused to immediate success at a sport and so frustrated with myself did I work so much to get better.

My original goal was simply not to stink at tennis. Fortunately for my ego and self-esteem, I got to be a pretty decent player fairly quickly, but the uniqueness of tennis had hooked me for good. It was a one-on-one deal out there. No substitutions, no timeouts, no coaching allowed, no clock running out to end a match. You could get out-hit, out-run, or out-thought; there were so many ways to win or lose. I took lessons; I read tennis books and magazines; I watched matches on television. I drove my parents nuts, I think.

Adding to my intrigue with the sport was that three blocks away, a kid two years younger was already playing an effortless, glorious, calculating brand of tennis with much less time spent on the court. His name was John McEnroe. I grew up with him. He did things by instinct that I spent many tedious hours trying to copy. He was a small boy for a long time—his nickname at the Douglaston Club was "Runt"—but time and again he'd beat kids bigger than he was, stronger by far, more dedicated, much older. He fascinated me.

I could never approach McEnroe's level, but I still wanted to be as good a tennis player as I could be. I wasn't nearly as gifted as John, but I was a good worker and played a pretty heady game of tennis. I got to play professionally for three years, but never without bad knees, and when I had to quit, I spent an awful lot of time wondering how I could have prevented my injuries. I think the reason I continue to love and be more fascinated by the game is because I somehow felt that I had more inside me to give—it has never left my system.

If you are reading this book, you've probably got tennis in you, too. Maybe you're already pretty good at it. Maybe you're a good jock, or maybe you're technically sound, or maybe you're a smart, canny competitor. Maybe you're all of the above, in which case you're on your way. But if you're lacking in some skills or want to be sure you're maximizing the skills you've got, read this book by Nick Bollettieri and Dr. Charles Maher. It is a serious, thoughtful, systematic approach to tennis. It will make you take stock of yourself and your game. It will help you to focus, revise, and rethink your efforts. It can create good habits for everything you try to accomplish, on or off the court.

The Mental Efficiency Program presented in this book is divided into a set of no-nonsense, very pragmatic chapters that challenge you to be your best. The implementation is practical and appropriate for players at all levels of the game. The procedures introduced here encourage consistent growth and problem-solving abilities.

If you are a serious tennis player, or if you want to be, use this book and accept the challenges it offers. You may find that you refer to it over and over again. If at book's end, you can say that you have done all the work and grasped all of the lessons therein, you will feel very good about yourself. You will not have wonder, as I still do, "What if...?"

PREFACE

This book is about mental efficiency, positive self-development, and you.

WHAT IS MENTAL EFFICIENCY?

Mental efficiency is the ability to use your thoughts and emotions to be the best at what you do. In the sport of tennis, mental efficiency involves coordination of how you think, feel, and act as you play tennis and as you take part in all other aspects of your life, such as school and work. In essence, mental efficiency contributes to the positive development of yourself.

The Mental Efficiency Program presented in this book teaches you how to be responsible for your own personal development. For the parent or teacher, it provides a guide to communicate information to your child or student that will help them to be their best at what they do. The Mental Efficiency Program allows you to focus on such positive things as competence building, individualized learning, and problem prevention. This is a forward-looking approach of applying psychology to sport—in this case the sport of tennis—and stands in contrast to the predominant focus whereby psychological methods are used after a player has developed performance or personal problems in achieving their best efforts.

Mental efficiency can be learned. It cannot, however, be forced on a tennis player through a set of narrow techniques. It is best fostered naturally in the learning and development of an individual person—built into training and practice sessions, at school, and in all daily living patterns. You (or your child or student) are, therefore, considered responsible for your own mental skills and personal growth. You are not merely a case study, but an active participant in the learning and development process—a proactive approach to sport psychology as opposed to today's reactive methods.

WHEN YOU ARE MENTALLY EFFICIENT

When you are mentally efficient, you are "in synch" with yourself. You are not wasting thoughts and emotions. Consequently, your physical actions, like hitting a backhand topspin passing shot, are likely to be more effective. When you are mentally efficient, you talk to yourself positively; you encourage yourself on and off the tennis court. You can easily visualize yourself performing well in competitive situations—in a crucial game or set.

Furthermore, you believe that you can reach another level with your game and achieve the skills it takes to do so. When you are mentally efficient, you also are not intimidated by an opponent; you quickly dispel fear, worry, and doubt about your play.

However, when you are not mentally efficient, you are likely to waste your thoughts and emotions. Examples of being inefficient mentally are talking negatively to yourself about how you play, imagining yourself committing many unforced errors, believing that you cannot win a match, and being intimidated by an opponent.

By being mentally efficient, you are in very sound personal position to prevent negative thoughts and emotions from occurring. You are more able to minimize them at their onset. By doing so, you help keep yourself in a positive state, while preventing performance and personal problems. You are better prepared and at a high level of personal performance to play up to your current level. You also develop the ability to be prepared in other sports and areas of your life. Overall, you enhance your positive self-development for tennis, sport, and life.

WHAT YOU WILL LEARN IN THIS BOOK

Through this book, you will learn about particular personal qualities, abilities, steps and activities. This information will help you become the best tennis player and person possible. It also will enable you to enjoy the process of your own self-development. As a result, you will be able to do the following:

◆ Understand your strong points, limitations, and needs for development in tennis and other areas of your life (Personal Awareness)

◆ Know what you want to accomplish in tennis and why you want to do so (Self-Motivation)

◆ Believe that you can execute on the court and perform well against your opponents (Self-Confidence)

◆ Prepare yourself thoroughly to play and follow through on your training regimen and goals (Self-Discipline)

◆ Develop worthwhile experiences with the people involved in your development (Quality Interpersonal Relationships)

◆ Regard yourself as a unique individual and worthwhile person (Self-Esteem)

◆ Use information about your performance to reach new game levels (Continuous Improvement)

THE CHAPTERS IN THIS BOOK

To acquire the above qualities and abilities, you can take certain steps and activities. These steps and activities make up the majority of this book. Following an introductory chapter, *Taking a Personal Perspective,* you will read chapters entitled:

- ◆ *Becoming Aware of Yourself*
- ◆ *Achieving Self-Motivation*
- ◆ *Building and Maintaining Self-Confidence*
- ◆ *Possessing Self-Discipline*
- ◆ *Maintaining Quality Interpersonal Relationships*
- ◆ *Developing Positive Self-Esteem*
- ◆ *Committing to Continuous Improvement*
- ◆ *Taking the Mental Efficiency Advantage*

HOW THE BOOK IS ORGANIZED

The chapters of the book are organized in a manner to provide you with the tools necessary to develop quickly and effectively. These chapters describe and discuss such things as personal qualities of mental efficiency, personal benefits that you will gain by possessing these qualities, along with personal problems that will be prevented. Relatedly, the chapters detail the steps to take and activities to complete in order to be a mentally efficient tennis player and person.

Each chapter consists of the basic text, as well as major points that have been pulled from the text and highlighted in the lefthand margins. The basic text provides the precise information that you can use to boost your mental efficiency. The highlight points in the margins can serve as benchmarks to help you make sure that you are learning the material.

As a lead-in to each chapter, a personal anecdote is included that has to do with the material that follows. Along with the chapter lead-ins, there are quotations from famous and successful people in tennis, sport, and life that correspond to chapter content. This material will help you focus your attention on the chapter and help maximize your learning.

Following the last chapter, we have included references that support the material presented in the chapters. At the end, we also have included an appendix that describes how we went about designing and implementing the Mental Efficiency Program.

Mental efficiency is a "total program approach" to playing tennis. The program combines every aspect of your life: tennis, school, study, family, and socialization. We encourage you not only to read this book, but to discuss it with your tennis coach, parents, and other individuals whom you trust and respect. We believe that you will be provided a solid foundation for tennis, sport, and life. Enjoy the process.

Nick Bollettieri
Dr. Charles Maher
September 1994

1

TAKING A

PERSONAL

PERSPECTIVE

The entrance to Victory Park, Nick's first teaching facility.

The quality of a person's life is in direct proportion to their commitment to excellence, regardless of their chosen field or endeavor.

Vince Lombardi
NFL Football Coach

To be what we are, and to become what we are capable of becoming, is the only end in life.

Robert Louis Stevenson
Scottish Novelist and Poet

It's so multifaceted that you can't play to the fullest until you've developed some maturity and sense of perspective on life.

Virginia Wade
Tennis Player, Commentator

When I graduated from Spring Hill College, my father wanted me to go to law school and was determined that I would become a lawyer. As a dutiful son, I applied to the University of Miami to complete my education.

I had no thoughts at the time that I wanted to be a tennis coach. During the summers and on a part-time basis, I began to teach at Victory Park in North Miami Beach. I had two courts and a cooler and umbrella for a pro shop—pretty meager beginnings.

As time went on, I began to feel that what I was doing on the court was more than just a summer job. I really felt that I had a "calling" to help people —especially young people—not only learn to be

1

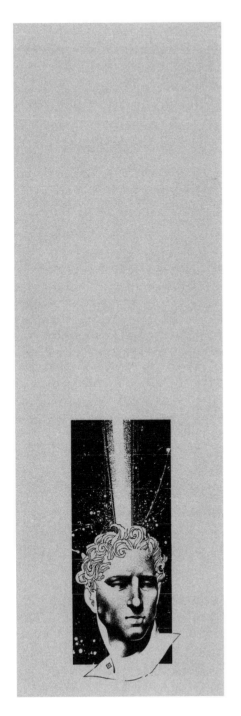

better tennis players, but also to be better people and to take tennis beyond the court and into their lives.

I knew that this "gift" was something much more important to me—and to others—than what I might be able to accomplish continuing in school. I had to make a decision, and I chose to follow my heart—it has never let me down.

I organized my goals and my time around building my "dream" into something well beyond Victory Park. I tried many things and had some failures, but along the way, I learned from each. Many people in the tennis business thought that my ideas were "whacko"—mass teaching, a boarding summer tennis camp, a full-time Academy with quality tennis and academics—but today they are the norm, rather than the exception.

Looking back, I know that I made the right decision, and I would do nothing differently. Although my dad had wanted me to pursue law, he always said, "Son, if you believe in it, do it." I made up my mind to stick to teaching, and I organized my life and priorities to accommodate this. In spite of all the stumbling blocks, my personal goals stayed firm. I took a personal perspective of my life and have never doubted my decision.

Nick Bollettieri

1 | TAKING A PERSONAL PERSPECTIVE

WHAT'S IN THIS CHAPTER

In this chapter, we introduce you to positive self-development and mental efficiency in tennis and describe the basic features of the Mental Efficiency Program.

We also suggest how you can read and use the information in the book to add value to yourself, as a tennis player and as a person.

THE BIG PICTURE

We encourage you to place yourself, as a tennis player, into a personal perspective. This bigger picture will help you recognize that tennis influences all aspects of your life just as events in your life influence your tennis development.

In this regard, consider yourself not only as a tennis player, but also as a unique individual who exists beyond the game. This personal perspective serves as the basis or foundation for your mental efficiency.

As you read this book, think about how the material applies not only to your tennis, but also to other parts of your life. These areas include school and college, family membership, the workplace, and community involvement.

Most of the individuals we know who play tennis and who

A bigger picture viewpoint will help you recognize that tennis influences all aspects of your life just as events in your life influence your tennis development.

Consider yourself not only as a tennis player, but also as a unique individual who exists beyond the game.

Tennis can be a very worthwhile part of growing up, a routine aspect of your life and a favorite pastime.

enjoy playing are able to take this kind of personal perspective—to be able to put themselves into the big picture. These individuals range from world class champions, to good collegiate level competitors, club players, high school participants, and those just starting to really learn the game.

Tennis has a longstanding, exciting tradition and history. It has evolved into a popular international sport. For some individuals, tennis has given them a source of professional livelihood. Yet, in its proper perspective, tennis can be so many other things to you. In particular, tennis can be a very worthwhile part of growing up, a routine aspect of your life and a favorite pastime.

Tennis can be a positive challenge, particularly when you view tennis—and enjoy it—as a game of rapid decisions and quick adjustments—both physical and mental.

However, when tennis is not viewed and enjoyed in this way, the natural tendency is for a player, including perhaps yourself, to become anxious, lose concentration, and to become disenchanted with the game.

By taking a personal perspective, the game of tennis will provide you with a range of personal development benefits.

By taking a personal perspective, the game of tennis will provide you with a range of personal development benefits. By taking a personal perspective, you will also be able to limit—or even eliminate—unwanted personal problems or negative states, such as anger. In essence, you will become and remain a mentally efficient tennis player and person.

POSITIVE SELF-DEVELOPMENT

Positive self-development involves adding value to yourself. This means getting progressively better at playing tennis and at contributing in other areas of your life like school, home, and community.

Positive self-development involves adding value to yourself.

In terms of your positive self-development, there are several personal qualities that will contribute to your mental efficiency. We refer to these personal qualities as:

◆ Personal Awareness

◆ Self-Motivation

◆ Self-Confidence

◆ Self-Discipline

◆ Quality Interpersonal Relationships

◆ Self-Esteem

◆ Continuous Improvement

We will briefly mention each of these qualities below. We will discuss them and the steps and activities to undertake in the following chapters.

◆ PERSONAL AWARENESS

Personal awareness means knowing your current strengths, limitations, and needs for improvement as a tennis player and person.

Personal awareness means knowing your current strengths, limitations, and needs for improvement as a tennis player and person. Personal awareness also means having a personal mission, or vision, for how you wish to proceed in tennis and other areas.

For example, you may know that your serve is a strong part of your game, but you need to improve your footwork if you are to be an effective serve and volley player. Or, you may believe that you have good concentration when you serve, but you recognize that you need to remain calm and better composed before match play and during changeovers.

Personal awareness is also important to aspects of your life beyond tennis. In particular, you can benefit by better understanding your strengths and needs in school and in your work or business.

By being personally aware, you are more focused and better able to make necessary changes and adjustments—both on and off the tennis court.

◆ SELF-MOTIVATION

Self-motivation has to do with your desire to seriously want to make progress toward and attain your personal goals.

Self-motivation has to do with your desire to seriously

To enhance your self-motivation, you can set personal goals that are specific and challenging to you and are ones that you really want to achieve.

want to make progress toward and attain your personal goals. These goals are similar for most people but will vary in degree and kind dependent on your skill development, needs, and desire.

For instance, your personal goals may have to do with the progress you are making at particular tennis skills, your performance in match play, or your development as a student in school.

When you are self-motivated, you have the desire and focus to do well. Personal desire and focus, however, do not come to you by chance nor are you born with them. Rather, you develop self-motivation when you play tennis for sound reasons—enjoying the commitment and challenges of sport rather than wanting to win awards, gain recognition, or to please others.

To enhance your self-motivation, you can set personal goals that are specific and challenging to you and are ones that you really want to achieve. Self-motivation is also an important personal quality for success at school, for participating as a valuable member of the family, in the community, or at work—for all areas of life.

Self-confidence encompasses the idea of trusting yourself – playing tennis in a relaxed and controlled way, without overanalyzing what you are doing as you perform.

◆ SELF-CONFIDENCE

Self-confidence involves believing that you can execute and perform well both on and off the tennis court. Furthermore, self-confidence is seen in your desire to overcome obstacles in development and maintain your poise and composure during competition.

In a sense, self-confidence encompasses the idea of trusting yourself—playing tennis in a relaxed and controlled way, without overanalyzing what you are doing as you perform.

Trusting yourself involves letting yourself go, while enjoying the process of practicing and playing tennis.

◆ SELF-DISCIPLINE

Self-discipline is being able to start your training with a defined goal and to follow through, making necessary adjustments along the way.

Self-discipline is being able to start your training with a defined goal and to follow through, making necessary adjustments along the way.

Self-discipline has to do with preparing for, and following through, in the short term—points, games, sets, matches, practice sessions, as well as long-range tennis goals. Self-discipline involves sticking with your plans, not giving in on them when things do not go your way, while remaining focused and poised.

In addition to tennis, self-discipline is an important quality for doing well in other areas of your life such as completing your course assignments, fulfilling family responsibilities, or starting a new business.

◆ QUALITY INTERPERSONAL RELATIONSHIPS

Your ability to experience quality interpersonal relationships occurs when you relate to other individuals and groups in mutually beneficial ways.

Your ability to experience quality interpersonal relationships occurs when you relate to other individuals and groups in mutually beneficial ways. This means that both you and those people with whom you are interacting receive something positive and worthwhile from the interchange.

For instance, this might be helpful with improving a tennis stroke, advice about strategy against a specific opponent, or developing a relationship with a coach or team.

Quality interpersonal relationships are seen in your cooperation with teammates, with a doubles partner, in listening to a friend, or in reviewing your match performance with your coach.

In other areas of your life, quality interpersonal relationships allow you to be respectful of teachers and peers, as well as to get along well with family members, including your parents, or an employer.

When you possess positive self-esteem, you view yourself as a unique individual, and you are happy about who you are and what you do.

Continuous improvement involves never being satisfied, nor wanting to stay put – always wanting to reach another level and be your best.

◆ SELF-ESTEEM

Self-esteem is the personal quality in which you regard yourself as a person in a positive way. When you possess positive self-esteem, you view yourself as a unique individual, and you are happy about who you are and what you do.

With self-esteem, you evaluate your own tennis performance objectively, noticing things that you have done well and not so well. You are able to regard yourself in this way because you do not equate your performance as a tennis player with yourself as a person.

For example, if you do not perform as expected—lose a match or make too many unforced errors—you have the ability to identify and separate that performance as something not acceptable to you, while still holding yourself as a person in high regard.

In contrast, when you do perform well, you accept it as a fact, feel good about the performance, but do not let it "go to your head."

◆ CONTINUOUS IMPROVEMENT

Continuous improvement involves your wanting to develop and refine your knowledge, skills, and abilities, both on and off the tennis court.

Continuous improvement involves never being satisfied, nor wanting to stay put—always wanting to reach another level and be your best. The focus is on becoming progressively better, adding to your tennis development and in other areas of your life and enjoying the process of playing, learning, and living.

MENTAL EFFICIENCY

Mental efficiency encompasses the seven personal qualities described above. Mental efficiency is a desired and very important aspect of your positive self-development. Mental efficiency has to do with your ability to coordinate your thoughts, emotions, and physical actions in the best manner possible as you practice and play tennis.

By being mentally efficient, you think productively, keep your emotions under proper control, and execute physically. Mental efficiency is important to all aspects of your development in tennis, from preparation for an upcoming match, to execution during a match, to having quality practice sessions, and for many other areas of your life (e.g., daily schedule, free time).

When you are mentally efficient, you remain balanced and in control.

POSITIVE RESULTS OF MENTAL EFFICIENCY

When you are mentally efficient, you remain balanced and in control. For instance, you can learn to talk to yourself positively when you begin to feel negative during a practice, stay focused on each point, and remain poised during a match.

In essence, when you are mentally efficient, you prevent needless waste of your energies—mental and physical.

As a result, by being mentally efficient, you are much more likely to have quality practices, follow through on your long-range goals, remain in a positive state for matches, keep your composure during competitive situations, and come back ready to work on your game even after a poor performance or unexpected loss.

When you are mentally efficient, you are personally aware, self-motivated, self-confident, self-disciplined, enjoy quality interpersonal relationships, possess high self-esteem, and seek to continuously improve yourself.

FUNCTION EFFICIENTLY AND EFFECTIVELY

When you are mentally efficient, you are personally aware, self-motivated, self-confident, self-disciplined, enjoy quality interpersonal relationships, possess high self-esteem, and seek to continuously improve yourself.

Consequently, you are able to function efficiently and effectively both on and off the court. You can do this because you are able to:

◆ Understand your strong points, limitations, and needs

In this book, we discuss how you can acquire and develop the personal qualities and acquire the abilities associated with mental efficiency in tennis.

for development in tennis and other areas of your life (Personal Awareness)

◆ Know what you want to accomplish in tennis and why you want to do so (Self-Motivation)

◆ Believe that you can execute effectively on the tennis court and perform well competitively (Self-Confidence)

◆ Prepare yourself thoroughly to play and to follow through on your goals (Self-Discipline)

◆ Make your contacts with people—coaches, teammates, media, etc.—quality experiences (Quality Interpersonal Relationships)

◆ Regard yourself as a unique individual and worthwhile person (Self-Esteem)

◆ Use information about your performance to improve your play (Continuous Improvement)

In the remainder of the book, we discuss how you can acquire and develop the personal qualities and acquire the abilities associated with mental efficiency in tennis. Before we do so, however, we want to provide you with an overview of the basic features of the Mental Efficiency Program. This will help you recognize what the program is and what it is not intended to be.

BASIC FEATURES OF THE MENTAL EFFICIENCY PROGRAM

The basic features of the Mental Efficiency Program are discussed below and outlined in the Mental Efficiency Program Summary Chart, as seen on page 12. This chart is divided into four columns:

◆ **Area/Quality** – This column lists the personal qualities associated with positive self-development and mental efficiency.

◆ **Ability** – This column describes what you are able to do when you are mentally efficient with respect to the area and the personal quality.

◆ **Benefits** – This column lists the positive things that you experience when you acquire and develop each personal quality and ability.

◆ **Problems Prevented** – This column lists the problems that you can prevent from occurring by being mentally efficient.

When you look at the chart from left to right, you will notice that each area or personal quality reflects an ability that you can acquire and develop. By learning and developing the specific quality and ability in each area, you will contribute to your overall mental efficiency.

By learning and developing the specific quality and ability in each area, you will contribute to your overall mental efficiency.

It is important to note from the chart that if you possess each ability, you will derive certain positive benefits and you will be much better equipped to prevent particular related problems from occurring. This is the proactive basis of mental efficiency.

These personal qualities, abilities, benefits, and problems apply not only to your tennis, but also to other areas of your life, although the primary focus of the following chapters and this book will be on tennis.

SEVEN RELATIONSHIPS

In essence, the chart points out seven relationships involved in being mentally efficient. These seven relationships can be considered the basic features of the Mental Efficiency Program. They are:

When you are personally aware, you understand your strong points, limitations, and needs for development as a tennis player and a person.

1 When you are **personally aware**, you understand your strong points, limitations, and needs for development as a tennis player and a person. Consequently, you benefit by possessing accurate and thorough knowledge about yourself. You have an overall vision of where you are now and where you want to be. Problems of confusion about yourself and lack of direction are curtailed and prevented.

Figure 1-1. Mental Efficiency Program Summary Chart

Area/Quality	Ability	Benefits	Problems Prevented
1. Personal Awareness	Understanding your strong points, limitations, and needs for development	Knowledge Vision	Confusion Lack of direction
2. Self-Motivation	Knowing what you want to accomplish and why you want to do so	Desire Focus	Disinterest Distractibility Boredom
3. Self-Confidence	Believing that you can execute effectively on the court and perform well against opponents	Personal trust Belief Poise	Fear Sense of inadequacy Intimidation
4. Self-Discipline	Preparing yourself thoroughly to play and following through on your game plans	Information Concentration Perseverance	Waste of time Loss of control Apathy
5. Quality Interpersonal Relationships	Making your contacts with people quality experiences	Cooperation Contribution Respect	Self-centeredness Neglect Disrespect
6. Self-Esteem	Regarding yourself as a unique and worthwhile person	Enjoyment Personal regard	Negativism Poor opinion of self
7. Continuous Improvement	Using information about your performance to improve your play	Action Change Enthusiasm	Complacency Stagnation Helplessness

When you are self-motivated, you know what you want to accomplish and why you want to do so.

When you are self-confident, you believe that you can execute effectively during training and competition.

Self-discipline allows you to concentrate more fully and to persevere despite obstacles and setbacks.

Quality interpersonal relationships with individuals involved in your development and training benefit you and are worthwhile experiences.

2 When you are **self-motivated**, you know what you want to accomplish and why you want to do so. With this information, you benefit by having the desire and focus to act on your motives.

Through self-motivation, you can prevent yourself from being disinterested in what you are doing, distracted by other things or other people, and becoming bored with yourself.

3 When you are **self-confident**, you believe that you can execute effectively during training and competition. In this regard, you benefit by trusting yourself, believing in what you are doing, and remaining poised. In so doing, you prevent feelings of fear, a sense of inadequacy, or being intimidated by opponents.

4 When you are **self-disciplined**, you have prepared yourself thoroughly to train and compete and to follow through on your goals as well as make any necessary adjustments along the way. As a result, you benefit by being ready and prepared with respect to what you are doing and what you might expect on the court (adjusting to playing conditions, to a specific opponent style, etc.).

This ability then allows you to concentrate more fully and to persevere despite obstacles and setbacks—preventing waste of time, a perception of loss of control, and feelings of apathy.

5 **Quality interpersonal relationships** with individuals involved in your development and training benefit you and are worthwhile experiences, for several reasons:

First, you will most likely receive cooperation from other people. This is a reciprocal process, and people who help you are also benefitting from this experience and relationship. Respect, admiration, and friendship are direct benefits to you.

Furthermore, you will be able to prevent self-centeredness, disrespect for others, irresponsibility, and isolation.

When you possess positive self-esteem, you regard yourself as a unique individual and worthwhile person no matter what the outcome is on the tennis court or in any other event in your life.

6 When you possess positive **self-esteem**, you regard yourself as a unique individual and worthwhile person no matter what the outcome is on the tennis court or in any other event that occurs in your life.

You are likely to benefit because you can more easily enjoy your daily experiences—including training and competitive play. You are able to hold yourself in high regard and in so doing can help to prevent problems of being negative about yourself, having little self-respect, or developing a poor opinion about yourself.

In terms of continuous improvement, you are able to use information about your performance in an objective manner to improve and reach another level of play.

7 In terms of **continuous improvement**, you are able to use information about your performance in an objective manner in order to improve and reach another level of play. You benefit because you are committed to personal actions and positive change, and you are enthusiastic about trying to reach another level of progress.

You are also able to prevent problems having to do with being complacent about your development, about sliding backward in your development (stagnation), or developing a feeling of helplessness.

READING AND USING THIS BOOK

We recommend that you read this book first in its entirety.

We recommend that you read this book first in its entirety. This will give you a good understanding of what mental efficiency is and how you can learn and benefit from being mentally efficient. You will also be able to ask questions and note any points that are unclear to you or that might require additional reading.

After reading the book completely, you should go back to each chapter and apply the steps, methods, and procedures on a regular basis. In Chapter 9, we provide you with a way to use the book and the Mental Efficiency Program on a regular basis.

Mental efficiency is a dynamic and ongoing process that

The more you involve the entire "team" – the player, the coach, and the parent – the more quickly and more effectively you will be able to become mentally efficient both as a tennis player and as a person.

will grow with you as you grow and develop both on and off the court.

You should also discuss mental efficiency with your coach, advisors, and parents. The more you involve the entire "team"—the player, the coach, and the parent—the more quickly and more effectively you will be able to become mentally efficient both as a tennis player and as a person.

2

BECOMING AWARE OF YOURSELF

Nick and Aaron Krickstein training during Aaron's rookie years on the professional circuit.

Aaron Krickstein came down to the Academy for the first time when he was just 14, accompanied by his father, Herb—a doctor, avid golfer, and very astute and powerful business man. Aaron was a very shy boy in every respect, both on and off the court. He was extremely tough on himself—shoulders slumped in play, private self-talks, head down, etc. And, being the only boy in a family with three sisters, he was very sheltered and protected.

He had all the tennis mechanical credentials, but such a negative self-esteem that he was very difficult to motivate in terms of teaching. He also had difficulty in relating to the other kids—not at all like Jimmy Arias and Carling Bassett, who were there at this same time. I couldn't yell or get upset in teach-

ing Aaron as I could with them. He would have broken down. He had to have positive reinforcement.

But I knew that if we could get Aaron to break out of this shell, he would be one of the best. I waited.

Ironically, it happened when we were together in Florence, Italy, at an event. He was about 16 years old and was with his dad, my son Jimmy, and me. Before the trip, my ex-wife Kellie and I had given Aaron a book, **The Road Less Traveled,** *by Scott Peck. The chapter headings and one quote that we had pointed out to him seemed to have a profound effect.*

He wouldn't put it down! It appeared to be a turning point and to have a great effect on his entire outlook on life. A book! After years of struggling to get him to believe in himself, the words that he read in this book did it for me. I'll never forget the lesson learned.

Today, Aaron and I are very close. We learned a lot from each other in this particular experience— about people and what it takes to become aware of one's self. Our mutual respect and sharing continues.

Nick Bollettieri

2 | BECOMING AWARE OF YOURSELF

WHAT'S IN THIS CHAPTER

Personal awareness refers to your ability to know yourself as a tennis player and as a person. When you possess this quality, you are aware of your strong points, limitations, and development needs.

This chapter focuses on personal awareness as a quality of a mentally efficient tennis player. We suggest appropriate activities for you to use to understand your strong points, limitations, and development needs.

STRONG POINTS, LIMITATIONS, AND DEVELOPMENT NEEDS

Strong points are the mental skills and physical skills that help you perform during training and competition. These include skills like concentration, relaxation, serve and volley skills, and others.

Limitations have to do with skills that you do not now possess, but need to have to improve your tennis game and performance. For example, to improve your forehand, you may be limited by slow footwork, which you will need to improve at the same time as you develop your forehand stroke.

Limitations also have to do with your physical makeup

Personal awareness refers to your ability to know yourself as a tennis player and as a person.

19

such as your height, weight, strength, coordination, and other physical factors that dictate or limit how you play ("playing within yourself").

Development needs reflect the specific mental and physical skills that you must work on to reach another level and become a better player. For example, you may need to develop your ability to concentrate on improving your first serve percentage.

Although you may already possess particular mental and physical skills and consider them as strong points, you still may need to develop them further in order to reach higher levels of performance. What is a strong point at one level of competitive match play, for instance your net play, becomes a need for development as you proceed to play more experienced opponents.

> **You can develop your strong points even further.**

WHY YOU NEED TO BE PERSONALLY AWARE

Developing a sound and thorough personal awareness— knowing yourself—will help you identify your strong points, limitations, and what you need to improve upon.

When you review this kind of information by yourself, and then when you discuss it with other people such as your tennis coach and/or parents, you are able to make better decisions about how to continue to improve your tennis play as well as other aspects of your life.

> **Developing a sound and thorough personal awareness – knowing yourself – will help you identify your strong points, limitations, and areas for improvement.**

These decisions will be made more easily and effectively because you will be able to formulate a "big picture" viewpoint of where you are now and where you want to go with your tennis game. As a result, you will contribute to your mental efficiency as a tennis player.

GAIN PERSONAL BENEFITS

You can gain several personal benefits by developing a complete awareness and understanding of yourself.

1 First, you will really learn about your strong points and needs for improvement. You can gain this knowledge by asking and answering questions about your tennis game, why you play, and what you need to do to get better.

This process of asking and answering questions allows you to focus on yourself and to be honest with yourself. In turn, this knowledge will help you remain motivated to get better.

2 Second, another benefit in becoming more personally aware of your strengths and needs is that you can plan and look ahead more accurately in deciding where you want to go with your game (goal setting) and how to prepare yourself (personal planning).

We have found that tennis players who can really formulate a clear image of themselves in terms of their roles and goals in tennis not only become excited at their vision, but are also more likely to follow through and achieve them.

For example, if you know your strong points and needs, and your goal is to attain a college tennis scholarship, the chances are that you will be able to plan more effectively and follow through on this goal with a vision of what you want to accomplish rather than without one.

PREVENT DISINTEREST IN THE GAME

You also can prevent several personal problems from affecting your game by having a complete awareness of yourself.

First, you will prevent yourself from becoming disinterested in playing and training. This will happen because you will have determined your strong points, limitations, and development needs.

Prevent disinterest by challenging yourself to be a better player. In doing so, it will be clear to you how to proceed in order to continue to improve and be the best player possible.

Focus and be honest with yourself.

You will be a better planner if you have a vision.

Prevent disinterest by challenging yourself to be a better player.

Focus on what is important and what you need to work on.

You will know where you want to go, and you will know precisely how to get there.

Over time, interests and desires other than playing tennis are likely to become clearer and more important to you and help to define your interest in tennis to a greater, equal, or lesser degree.

PREVENT DISTRACTIONS

A second problem that you can prevent by having a thorough awareness of yourself is that you will not be distracted by things or people that do not contribute to your progress and performance. For instance, taking a school examination the day before a big tournament would not be significantly distracting to you.

Without personal awareness, distractions are likely to occur simply because you are not clear with yourself about what is important and what you need to do to achieve the results you want.

When you are personally aware of yourself, the chances are that you are less likely to focus on things that may be appealing and distract you from realizing the goals that you have set for yourself.

For example, you will be more aware of a particular need for improvement, such as learning a topspin lob. With this knowledge, it can be expected that you would allow yourself sufficient time to learn and practice this new stroke.

**Step 1
Develop an understanding of your strong points, limitations, and needs for improvement.**

Step 1

Develop an understanding of your strong points, limitations, and needs for improvement.

By taking this first step, your chances of developing a thorough awareness of yourself will be greatly increased, which, in turn, contributes to your overall mental efficiency. To learn this as both a tennis player and person, there are several activities that we recommend you undertake and complete.

It is important that you engage in these activities on a regular basis at the beginning of your training program and throughout the year.

These activities are:

1. Obtain information about yourself.

2. Profile yourself.

3. Discuss your personal profile with other people.

4. Write a personal mission statement.

5. Keep learning about yourself.

These activities are discussed in this chapter.

1. Obtain information about yourself.

You can obtain information about yourself by asking yourself focused questions.

You can obtain information about your strong points, limitations, and development needs as a tennis player and person by asking and answering some very important and focused questions.

In this way, you will obtain specific information that will enable you to create a profile of yourself which will allow you to focus on and better understand yourself.

Ask yourself focused questions

You can ask several basic questions about yourself as a tennis player and person.

These basic questions are:

◆ What are my current strong points?

- Tennis skills (both physical and mental)

- Physical fitness and condition

- Daily living skills

◆ What do I need to improve on to develop as a tennis player and person?

- Tennis skills (both physical and mental)
- Physical fitness and condition
- Daily living skills

◆ What is limiting my tennis and personal development that I need to prevent from occurring

- Limited knowledge about myself
- Ineffective or infrequent training
- Improper or inappropriate attitudes

The Tennis Skills Inventory is divided into both mental and physical tennis skills.

Complete the Tennis Skills Inventory

There are methods that have been devised to help you answer the above questions about your strong points, limitations, and needs for improvement.

We recommend that you complete this instrument by yourself.

Figure 2-1 displays the Tennis Skills Inventory. We recommend that you complete this inventory by yourself. When you do so, give yourself sufficient time to think seriously about your responses.

As you will see, the Tennis Skills Inventory is divided into various skill areas encompassing both the physical and mental aspects of the game. These areas are groundstroke play, transition play, net play, return of serve, movement, specialty shots, serve, style of play, and mental approach and skills.

Rate yourself on the Tennis Skills Inventory

Discuss your profile with your coach and others.

Once you have responded to the Tennis Skills Inventory, you will be able to use the results to help construct a profile of yourself and to discuss this information with your coach and/or your parents.

Complete the Physical Fitness and Condition Rating Scale

Rate your physical fitness skills: stamina, speed, strength, mobility, weight, and diet.

Figure 2-2 is entitled the Physical Fitness and Condition

Figure 2-1. Tennis Skills Inventory

In the space to the left of each item below, rate your level of skill development, as you believe it is at the current time. Use this scale for each item:

1 = Excellent   2 = Good   3 = Average   4 = Fair   5 = Poor

Groundstroke Play
_2_ 1. Forehand crosscourt
_3_ 2. Forehand down the line
_3_ 3. Backhand crosscourt
_4_ 4. Backhand down the line
_4_ 5. Backhand lob
_3_ 6. Forehand lob
_3_ 7. Forehand inside out

Transition Play
_2_ 1. Forehand approach shot crosscourt
_3_ 2. Forehand approach shot down the line
_3_ 3. Backhand approach shot crosscourt
_4_ 4. Backhand approach shot down the line

Net Play
_3_ 1. Forehand volley crosscourt
_3_ 2. Forehand volley down the line
_4_ 3. Backhand volley crosscourt
_4_ 4. Backhand volley down the line
_2_ 5. Overhead

Return of Serve
_2_ 1. Forehand in the deuce court
_4_ 2. Backhand in the deuce court
_3_ 3. Forehand in the ad court
_3_ 4. Backhand in the ad court

Movement
_2_ 1. To the wide forehand
_3_ 2. To the wide backhand
_2_ 3. To the short forehand
_2_ 4. To the short backhand
_2_ 5. On approach shots
_4_ 6. On volleys
_2_ 7. For overheads

Specialty Shots
_4_ 1. Forehand angle crosscourt
_4_ 2. Backhand angle crosscourt
_4_ 3. Forehand drop shot
_5_ 4. Backhand drop shot
_4_ 5. Forehand touch volley
_5_ 6. Backhand touch volley

Serve
_3_ 1. First serve flat
_4_ 2. First serve slice
_5_ 3. First serve topspin
_5_ 4. Second serve slice
_5_ 5. Second serve topspin

Style of Play
_3_ 1. Serve volley
_2_ 2. Aggressive baseliner
_2_ 3. Baseliner
_4_ 4. All court game

Mental Approach and Skills
_1_ 1. Setting personal goals
_2_ 2. Monitoring progress toward my goals
_1_ 3. Wanting to play competitively
_1_ 4. Enjoying the game
_4_ 5. Believing I can create shots and strategy
_2_ 6. Concentration and attention
_4_ 7. Maintaining poise
_2_ 8. Preparing for matches
_1_ 9 Having quality practices
_1_ 10. Getting along with coaches
_1_ 11. Getting along with teammates
_5_ 12. Not getting down on myself
_1_ 13. Committed to improvement
_1_ 14. Remaining motivated

Figure 2-2. Physical Fitness and Condition Rating Scale

In terms of your physical strength and condition, consider the following categories: stamina, speed, strength, mobility, weight, and diet.

For each category, rate yourself in reference to the respective items in the spaces to their left. Rate what you believe is your current level of development. Use this rating scale:

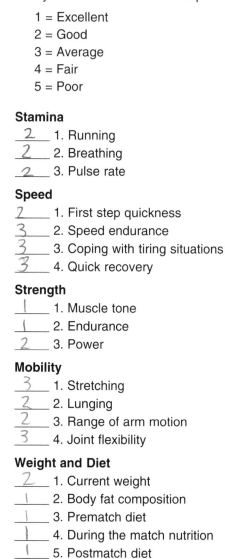

1 = Excellent
2 = Good
3 = Average
4 = Fair
5 = Poor

Stamina
_2_ 1. Running
_2_ 2. Breathing
_2_ 3. Pulse rate

Speed
_2_ 1. First step quickness
_3_ 2. Speed endurance
_3_ 3. Coping with tiring situations
_3_ 4. Quick recovery

Strength
_1_ 1. Muscle tone
_1_ 2. Endurance
_2_ 3. Power

Mobility
_3_ 1. Stretching
_2_ 2. Lunging
_2_ 3. Range of arm motion
_3_ 4. Joint flexibility

Weight and Diet
_2_ 1. Current weight
_1_ 2. Body fat composition
_1_ 3. Prematch diet
_1_ 4. During the match nutrition
_1_ 5. Postmatch diet

Rating Scale. You can use this rating scale in the same way that you did the Tennis Skills Inventory. In doing so, you will obtain information about your physical fitness and condition that you can compare with actual physical fitness data from your trainer or coach.

Rate your daily living activities and personal routines.

Fill out the Daily Living Skills Checklist

Figure 2-3, Daily Living Skills Checklist, will allow you to obtain information about your skills, abilities, and patterns in several areas that relate to your tennis performance and development. On the checklist, these areas are labeled School, Family and Community, and Personal Routines.

When you have rated yourself in these areas, you can use the information to help determine where you are strong and where you need to improve.

Complete the Personal Limitations Survey

Learn what has prevented you from doing as well as you would like to have done in tennis or in other areas of your life.

You can provide your opinions about what you think are your current limitations by completing the survey presented in Figure 2-4, entitled Personal Limitations Survey. In doing so, you will become more aware of factors that have prevented you from doing as well as you would like to have done, both on and off the tennis court.

In addition, by completing this survey, you will be more aware of factors that you have no control over changing such as your height. This, in turn, helps you to become more mentally efficient while preparing for and playing tennis.

Figure 2-3. Daily Living Skills Checklist

With respect to your daily living, consider the following dimensions: School, Family and Community, and Personal Routines. For each of these dimensions, rate yourself in reference to the items and skills under each category. In this regard, rate yourself in terms of how well you are doing at the current time. You can place your ratings on the spaces provided.

Use this rating scale: 1 = Excellent
                                 2 = Good
                                 3 = Average
                                 4 = Fair
                                 5 = Poor

School

_____ 1. Science and mathematics

___3___ 2. English and language arts

___3___ 3. Social studies

___2___ 4. Study skills

_____ 5. Completion of classwork and homework

Family and Community

___—___ 1. Relationships with brothers and sisters

___2___ 2. Quality of parent contacts

___2___ 3. Involvement in recreational experiences

___2___ 4. Follow-through on home chores and responsibilities

___—___ 5. Community participation (e.g., business, volunteer)

Personal Routines

___2___ 1. Productive use/scheduling of my time

___2___ 2. Coping with stressful life situations (e.g., relationships with people, death of someone close)

___1___ 3. Social skills

___1___ 4. Financial planning and direction

___3___ 5. Balancing tennis and other areas of life

Figure 2-4. Personal Limitations Survey

By responding to the questions below, you will learn more about what has
prevented you from doing better in tennis and other areas. Then, you can use
this information to do something to eliminate or minimize these limitations.

When you answer these questions, consider yourself in relation to the past
6 months to 1 year.

1. What information do I lack that may help me improve how I play tennis
   (e.g., how to apply mental skills; how to get along with other people;
   court strategy and tactics, other)?
   Experience, match play. How to apply mental skills, concentration

2. What factors—personal or otherwise—have hindered how I have performed (e.g., lack of practice; concern with obtaining awards; arguing
   with my coach)?
   *Lack of practice, late bloomer, having to financially
   back myself. Not enough time to devote fully to my sport
   until summer*

3. Are there any other things that come to mind that have hindered my
   play and that I can do something constructive about?
   *Hard life as a youngster. End work in June and
   see if concentrating solely on Tennis helps. Concentrate more
   on tennis (May-Aug) then physical training*

2. Profile yourself.

Once you have obtained information about yourself by answering the questions contained in the various testing checklists and scales described in the last section, you now are in position to create a personal profile of yourself.

Steps to Creating Your Personal Profile

You can create your personal profile by following the steps below.

Step 1

Identify your strong points.

Review the information that you have obtained from the various testing instruments to identify what you consider to be your strong points. If you gave yourself ratings of "excellent" or "good" on any items, these areas can be considered your strengths.

Place your strong points in the space provided on the Personal Profile Form (Figure 2-5) on page 31. Be sure that you have honestly answered the questions on this form about your strong points and that you have considered yourself in relation to all areas: tennis skills, physical fitness and condition, and daily living skills.

Step 2

Determine the areas that you need to develop.

Review the information to determine areas that you need to develop so that you can perform and function more effectively in tennis. A development need refers to knowledge, a skill, or an attitude that you need to acquire or improve upon to continue to make progress as a tennis player.

It is important for you to recognize here that a strong point that you have at one level of play (e.g., a backhand volley) may require refinement in terms of style and techniques for you to be effective at the next level of ability. Your strong point now, therefore, can become a development need.

Figure 2-5. Personal Profile Form

Name _Jack Gottlieb_   Date_____

My current strong points are (specify tennis skills, both physical and mental; physical fitness and condition; daily living skills):

1. Mental skills   Sociable
2. movement   independant
3. Forehand   masculine
4. overhead   desive
5. overall conditioning determination
                        Serving mechanics

My current needs for development are (specify tennis skills, both physical and mental; physical fitness and condition; daily living skills):

1. Serve (Slice, topspin) Volley(BH)
2. backhand   Slice approach shots
3. FH, angles
4. drop shots
5. maintaing pase

Personal limitations that I need to identify for improvement or elimination are (particular knowledge, skills, attitudes):

1. Get more experience In match play (singles)
2. maintaining pase
3. Just need time and people to help me improve, I can get to a higher level
4. Strategy improvement
5.

I plan to discuss my profile with _Kutztown Tennis coach_____.

List your needs for development on the Personal Profile Form.

This understanding and focus can then help you to continue to improve, not become complacent or "rest on your laurels."

If you have given yourself relatively low ratings on any of the items on the testing instruments, like ratings of "fair" and "poor," you may have identified development needs for yourself. Now consider all of the information and list your needs for development on the Personal Profile Form as described in Figure 2-5.

Step 3

Use the information about yourself to identify current personal limitations. A personal limitation refers to some factor (knowledge, skill, attitude) that has prevented you from doing as well as expected and that can be worked on (and in time eliminated) by identifying the limitation as a development need.

Identify and determine your current personal limitations.

You also can record information about your personal limitations on the Personal Profile Form (Figure 2-5).

Review your profile

At this point, you have completed a personal profile of yourself. This profile describes your strong points, limitations, and needs for development as a tennis player.

In reviewing the completed profile, ask yourself the following questions:

◆ To what extent do I believe the information that I have summarized about myself is accurate?

◆ If the information is accurate, what am I basing my judgments on besides my own opinion (e.g., performance data; coach ratings; feedback from others)?

◆ If the information is not accurate or not complete, what can I do to make it more accurate?

Based on your response to these questions, you may need

to complete one or more of the testing instruments more thoughtfully or consider other information about your performance that you have previously overlooked.

3. Discuss your personal profile with other people.

Get an outside check on the accuracy of your personal opinions.

Once you have profiled your personal strengths, limitations, and development needs, you can discuss that information with other people such as your tennis coach, parents, and perhaps a school teacher or advisor/mentor.

The reason for discussing this information with others is to obtain an "outside check" on the accuracy of your opinions. This method of discussion will also help to identify other things about your tennis skills, physical fitness and condition, or daily living skills that you have not considered about yourself. For instance, your coach may think that you have overrated yourself on your groundstroke skill ratings and underrated yourself on the quality of your serve.

In this case, you can discuss further with your coach the basis for his or her opinion. You may then want to add one or two items as development needs for yourself and adjust your strengths and limitations.

A personal mission statement outlines what you want to do as both a tennis player and person over the next two years.

Similar kinds of discrepancies may be identified when you discuss your physical fitness and condition, as well as your daily living patterns with other people—a fitness trainer or nutrition expert and others who know you.

4. Write a personal mission statement.

Writing a personal mission statement is helpful because it condenses even further important information about yourself. This helps make you more aware of yourself and helps you to be more mentally efficient.

You may want to pull all of the information that you now have about yourself into a summary form. You can do this by writing a personal mission statement.

A personal mission statement is a paragraph or several sentences in which you "talk to yourself" about what you want to do as a tennis player and person during the next year or two. Then, you write down what you have said to yourself.

Make your statement broad and meaningful

Your personal mission statement should be broad and meaningful for you. Here is an example of a personal mission statement written by an up and coming junior player:

Be sure that your mission statement is broad-based and clear.

"During the next two years, I want to graduate from high school and play college tennis on a scholarship. I want to improve my overall tennis game as well as increase my footwork and upper body strength. I want to improve my sectional ranking. I enjoy playing tennis, know that it benefits me, and want to continue to play."

As you will see by reviewing the above personal mission statement, you will be able to establish a broad-based, yet clear, perspective on what you want to do, when, and why.

Leave out self-centered reasons

In writing a personal mission statement, focus on things that have to do with the process of playing tennis and on your growth and development as a player and person.

Your mission statement should not refer to external, self-centered achievements.

A personal mission statement should not refer to external, self-centered achievements like trophies, getting your name in the paper, and having all people like you. This is because these external reasons will be short-lived or not possible, or to sustain you over time.

Enhance your positive self-development

You can use a personal mission statement to help enhance your positive self-development and mental efficiency in a variety of ways.

1 You can place a copy of your personal mission statement in a location where you will see it and think about it on a routine basis. This place may be in your room, a locker, over a desk where you work regularly—anywhere you will be exposed to it. This place should be a private location, not open to the general public. A mission statement is for personal use and for your benefit alone. It is not meant to be made public or an item for discussion by others.

A mission statement is for your own personal use and benefit and not for discussion by others.

2 Whenever you look at a copy of your mission statement, you can take a few moments every so often to think about or visualize yourself realizing your mission.

You can encourage yourself to see yourself following through on your goals, putting in quality practices, maintaining your composure during a match, discussing strategy with your coach and a host of other things that pertain to your mission.

Visualize yourself realizing your mission.

Change your mission statement when necessary

You can change your personal mission statement anytime you sense yourself losing a focus on your goals and plans, when you start getting down on yourself, or when new things emerge about your strong points, limitations, and development needs. The personal mission statement can serve as a source of inspiration to you and a means to enhance your personal awareness and mental efficiency. By changing your mission statement, you are growing.

Update your personal awareness profile two to three times a year.

5. Keep learning about yourself.

From time to time—perhaps two or three times a year— you can schedule a time with yourself to update your personal awareness.

In doing so, you will remain sharp and focused and continue to enjoy what you are doing. You will grow and better know yourself as a tennis player and person.

CHAPTER SUMMARY

In this chapter, we have focused on personal awareness as a quality of a mentally efficient tennis player. We have discussed the need for you to be personally aware of your strengths, limitations, and needs with respect to your tennis development and performance.

We then discussed Step 1 of the Mental Efficiency Program: Develop an understanding of your strong points, limitations, and needs for improvement.

Finally, we detailed how to proceed in developing a sound personal awareness through several separate, yet interrelated activities:

◆ Obtain information about yourself.

◆ Profile yourself.

◆ Discuss your personal profile with other people.

◆ Write a personal mission statement.

◆ Keep learning about yourself.

With this material as a basis, we will now focus on the area of self-motivation in the next chapter.

3

ACHIEVING

SELF-MOTIVATION

Nick in the early years at the Colony Beach & Tennis Resort on Longboat Key, Florida, with a crop of junior champions.

Much good work is lost for the lack of a little more.

E.H. Harriman
American Railway Magnate

Even if you're on the right track, you'll get run over if you just sit there.

Will Rogers
American Humorist

Desire is the key to motivation, but it's the determination and commitment to an unrelenting pursuit of your goal—a commitment to excellence—that will enable you to attain the success you seek.

Mario Andretti
Race Car Champion

Once I began to work with juniors—first at Victory Park in North Miami Beach and then at our first boarding summer camp in Beaver Dam, Wisconsin, now in its 27th year—I knew that I had a God-given gift to help them become their very best. But I also knew that if I were to be able to help juniors reach their goals, I would have to be with them more often—every day—and in a situation where they would have the chance to concentrate on their tennis goals and dreams.

I knew that this place would have to be a safe environment, and we would have to find a top academic facility that complemented our tennis programs.

I was incensed with achieving this dream—it

37

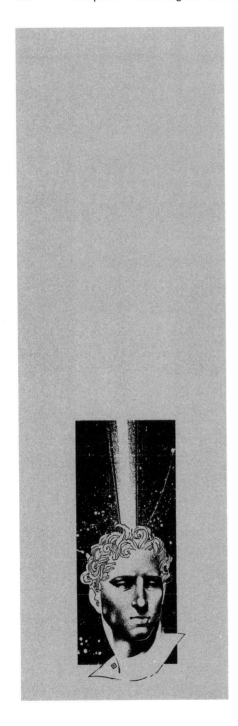

was a burning desire, but it had many obstacles in its path. The critics (and there were many of them) said that it was unhealthy and would never work. They said kids had to be in the home environment, with the local coach one-on-one, traveling with the parents or private coach, etc.

I also needed the financial assistance to carry it off. As had been so true in the past, my friends believed in me above and beyond the idea itself. They knew me well enough to know that if I wanted it badly enough, it was going to happen. So I kept pressing.

We had outgrown The Colony on Longboat Key, my personal home and the houses that we rented, and finally, the motel and club on 75th Street. We began an earnest search for larger space in the Bradenton area. What we found was an old tomato farm. We bought it and started moving ground. We were labeled as completely nuts; a hard-nosed paratrooper demanding discipline and excellence from young children. We had so many ups and downs that I felt like I was on a roller coaster.

At times, nothing seemed to work, but I was "hellbent" on making my dream come true even though it could have put me in the "looney bin." It's hard to comprehend that we would have gone to such extremes to get the place built, but there was no way I was going to give it up without trying.

The rest is history. From those old tomato vines have grown some of the finest talent in the history of the game and the world's largest and most sophisticated tennis training operation ever.

Nick Bollettieri

3 | ACHIEVING SELF-MOTIVATION

WHAT'S IN THIS CHAPTER

When you are self-motivated, you have the interest and desire to attain important goals.

Self-motivation is the personal quality associated with mental efficiency that helps you stay interested and active in what you do both on and off the tennis court. Motives are referred to as goals. When you are self-motivated, you have the interest and desire to attain important goals.

Therefore, these goals help you initiate effective actions. These goals and actions keep you focused on what you want to accomplish as a tennis player, why you want to do so, and how you will proceed to attain your goals. It is in this way that self-motivation contributes to your mental efficiency.

In this chapter, we discuss how you can reach a self-motivated state to become the best tennis player and person possible. You will learn how to motivate yourself to do a quality job during practice sessions and training, during match play, and to learn new aspects of your game.

The more personally aware of yourself that you are, the more self-motivated you will be.

Through the material presented in this chapter, you will learn to appreciate that self-motivation is a personal quality that is based on—and builds from—your level of personal awareness.

The more personally aware of yourself that you are, the more self-motivated you will be. This is the case because you will become aware of specific goals and actions upon which to act.

NEED FOR SELF-MOTIVATION

In defining self-motivation, we are referring to two important characteristics about an individual.

Self-motivation means that you have taken the personal initiative to set goals for yourself and to do what is necessary to attain them.

1 First, the self-motivated tennis player has what is called a "motive"—a reason for doing something in order to improve their overall game—reach another level of play.

This motive usually takes the form of a goal—preferably a written goal—and one that is specific, measurable, and attainable.

2 Second, the tennis player has decided to pursue his or her goal—take the necessary actions to reach the goal—such as practicing a specific shot. When this happens, a player is said to be motivated (i.e., motive for action).

When we say that a player is self-motivated, we mean that the individual has taken the personal initiative to set one or more goals and to initiate the necessary actions to attain them.

MAKE TENNIS YOUR OWN GAME

When you're self-motivated, you will enjoy all aspects of tennis more and welcome the challenges of training and competing. In developing this self-motivation, you will also be more interested in improving your game and in staying with the sport of tennis in spite of difficult times or setbacks.

You do not want other people to be your primary source of motivation.

When you are "burning with the desire" to do well and improve at tennis and other areas, you are relying on yourself and not waiting to be motivated by other people such as your coach or parents. Motivation that is not self-driven is a meager and short-lived motivation. While you certainly want help, guidance, and encouragement from other people, you do not want them to be your primary source of motivation.

If other people are the reason that you play tennis, the desire for you to do well or sustain your interest will be short-lived. This is because real enjoyment for doing something—like playing tennis in a quality way—comes primarily from within yourself. Playing tennis for yourself rather than for other people is a hallmark of mental efficiency for tennis, sport, and life.

IT'S UP TO YOU

You get excited and feel good when you "watch" yourself progress, develop new skills, cope effectively with difficult game situations, and advance to higher levels of performance.

Coaches, teachers, parents, and other people can help set the conditions for your improved performance. They can do this by providing you with information, equipment, facilities, and time, but only you can take advantage of these opportunities or create new ones on your own initiative.

GAIN PERSONAL BENEFITS

You will gain two major benefits by being able to motivate yourself effectively.

1 The first personal benefit is developing the desire to want to do well and to accomplish important goals that will make you a better player.

Desire is instilled in you because your motive for action comes primarily from within you, not from an external source. This kind of "within person desire"—self-driven—helps you to want to continue to perform and make progress even when things do not always go as you expected.

2 The second personal benefit from self-motivation is developing an increased focus about the things that make a difference for you in terms of your progress and performance. In particular, you will come to appreciate the value

Others can help you set conditions for improvement, but they can't make you take advantage of them.

Desire is instilled in you because your motive for action comes primarily from within you, not from an external source.

Develop an increased focus on what is important to you both on and off the tennis court.

of proper and appropriate attitudes, habits, and skills.

These things are referred to and discussed in this chapter as your personal goals. These personal goals have to do with processes—how you think, feel, and act—not only on a daily basis but over weeks and months in your training and development.

PREVENT PROBLEMS

By being self-motivated, you also are better able to identify and solve problems in your tennis game, your training, and in competition before these problems occur.

1 First, you are better able to prevent yourself from becoming disinterested and losing touch with what you are doing and why you are doing it, during practice and over the long term in tennis.

2 Second, by being self-motivated, you can prevent needless distractions (e.g., noises in crowd, weather, call by umpires) because what is important to you will be clear in your mind and you will have the desire to focus on it.

3 Third, you can prevent physical fatigue, boredom, and feelings of being "burned out." These psychological conditions are known to develop very subtly over time.

These negative states develop because the motives for action that direct and drive an individual in a positive way are missing. In essence, there is nothing for the individual to focus on or to take actions toward. Eventually, these people stop following through and become inactive and dissatisfied.

Step 2

Know what you want to accomplish and why.

There are several activities that you can undertake to help

> When you are self-motivated, you have positive energy that will help you control all aspects of your training.

> Being self-motivated allows you to block out negative distractions.

> Being self-motivated will give you more physical and mental energy.

you get to know what you want to accomplish in tennis and why you want to do so.

These activities are ones that you can follow through on continually throughout the year. You should do them on a routine basis, at least once a month.

The activities that will assist you in becoming and remaining self-motivated for tennis and other areas are the following:

1. Identify personal goals for yourself.

2. Make a commitment to your goals.

3. Discuss your goals with other people.

4. Monitor the progress you make toward your goals.

5. Use visualization.

6. Use positive affirmations.

Identify your personal goals.

Each of these activities will be discussed in the remainder of this chapter.

1. Identify personal goals for yourself.

In the chapter on personal awareness, we discussed how you can identify your strong points, limitations, and development needs.

We also showed you how to write a personal mission statement in order to give yourself a "big personal picture" of where you want to go with tennis and the related areas of your life.

Now, you can use the information and mission statement to identify personal goals that will serve as a primary source of self-motivation for you.

What is a personal goal?

A personal goal has to do with something important that relates to how you play tennis and perform at it. A personal goal has to do with your thoughts, emotions, and physical actions as a tennis player. A personal goal has meaning to you because if you progress toward the goal and attain it, the likelihood is increased that you will want to continue to play and develop your game.

Examples of personal goals

Below are four examples that illustrate personal goals with respect to the serve:

A personal goal has meaning to YOU.

- ◆ To learn to hit a higher percentage of first serves
- ◆ To keep my second serve deeper in the court and to my opponent's backhand
- ◆ To learn an effective "kick" serve
- ◆ To maintain my feeling of confidence even when my serve is broken

The drive from within

You will be able to remain self-motivated when your goals are ones that YOU can control.

It is important to mention here that you will sustain your efforts toward a goal—remain self-motivated—when the goal has to do with processes that are under your control (thoughts, emotions, physical actions).

This kind of personal goal stands in contrast to externally-focused objectives or outcomes. An example of this type of goal would be one in which your attention is focused on things generally outside your control and that are short-lived in terms of enhancing your self-motivation. These include things like trophies, having your name listed in the newspaper, and praise from some people.

The driving force to attain a goal, over the long term, comes not from outside yourself but from within yourself.

Identify your personal goals

To identify your personal goals, we recommend that you use the information you already have obtained about yourself, including the personal profile that you developed on yourself in Chapter 2, Becoming Aware of Yourself.

This includes information about yourself from the following areas:

Create a master list of goals and select the ones that are especially important for YOU to focus on.

◆ Tennis skills (physical and mental)

◆ Physical fitness and condition

◆ Daily living skills

Use the Identification List

Once you have reviewed this information, you then can identify particular goals and list those goals on Figure 3-1, Personal Goals Identification List.

In this way, you can create a "master list" of goals from which you can select particular ones to focus on.

2. Make a commitment to your goals.

Once you have identified your personal goals by placing them on a master list, you can now select the most important ones as goals that you are willing to make a commitment to.

Select enough goals so that you can stay focused and motivated.

Therefore, you are encouraged to (1) select enough goals so that you can stay focused and motivated and (2) use the following procedures in committing to your personal goals:

Select your goals

Use your master list of goals that you recorded on the Personal Goals Identification List (Figure 3-1).

From this list, decide on five or six goals. These goals should be ones that are most important at the present time to your development as a tennis player and your performance.

Choose the goals that are most important to you and use the master list of goals from the Personal Goals Identification List.

In making these goal selections, this does not mean that the other goals on your list are not important and that you do not need to expend effort to attain them. On the contrary, you need to work on these as well. However, the goals that you have selected are just a higher priority for you at this time.

Figure 3-1. Personal Goals Identification List

Name _Jack Gottlieb_   Date _4 /a/9?_

Tennis Skills Goals
1. Developing backhand —
2. Consistent valleys, development of BH valley —
3. Fine tune my forehand, develop semi western grip —
4. develop bh approach shot (slice)
5. dropshots - baseline and net —
6. develop all around serve —
7. get mentally tough, more experience —
8. developing all court game

Physical Fitness and Condition Goals —
1. develop more speed
2. flexibility
3. continuous strength training
4. using other resources

Daily Living Skills Goals
1. balancing tennis and other areas of life

Place your goals on the Personal Goals Form

Use the Personal Goals Form to record your goals.

Once you have decided on a set of five or six personal goals, you can place them on the Personal Goals Form, Figure 3-2 on page 48.

On this form, you should include your name and a description of your style of play (e.g., serve and volley, aggressive baseliner, baseliner, all-court game).

Next, include the date you are setting the goals and the time you expect to evaluate your progress in attaining them.

Sample goals provide guide

Table 3.1, on page 49, presents examples of the types of personal goal statements that pertain to your tennis and personal development. In reviewing this table, please remember that these are sample goals that will require more specification. This will be further discussed in the next section.

How many goals?

Select no less than three or four goals and no more than six or seven at any one time.

In identifying personal goals and selecting your most important ones, we suggest that you should select no less than three or four and no more than six or seven at any one time.

This does not mean, however, that you do not work on other goals and seek to make progress toward them. Rather, the ones that you have selected for personal focus are ones that are especially meaningful to your development and that need to be addressed in a planned and documented manner.

Figure 3-2. Personal Goals Form

Name _Jack Gottlieb_ _____ Style of play _All court_ _____

Date goal set _4/10/97_ _____

Evaluation date _6/9/97_ _____

Rating Scale
1 = Excellent
2 = Good
3 = Average
4 = Fair
5 = Poor

Personal Goals   **Progress Rating**

_4/16_

1. Developing Bachand (down the line and cross court, topspin,

2. Fine tune Forehand, develop semi-western grip, short ball' Eastern FH 'baseline

3. continue expanding my fitness level ST, CR ISO, Run etc...

4. develop power and variety on serve 1st serve % ?

5. bettering I can create shots and hit winner especially ability to hit serve

6. more consistency on volleys

Comments:

Use this table as a sample for your own goal statements.

Table 3.1
Selective Examples of Personal Goal Statements in Various Categories Having to Do with Tennis and Personal Development

Mechanical
- ◆ To improve the accuracy of my first serve
- ◆ To increase the percentage of my service return
- ◆ To get more depth on my ground stroke rallies
- ◆ To win more first points in a game
- ◆ To improve my fitness so that I can perform fully in long matches
- ◆ To add variety to my second serve

Mental
- ◆ To relax better on important points
- ◆ To become more disciplined in preparing for my matches
- ◆ To remain focused in between sets

Make each of your goals SMART to enhance your commitment to them.

Make Each Goal SMART

Now, you are ready to make each goal SMART. In this regard, SMART stands for a set of goal characteristics that will help you commit to them.

This means that you make sure that each of your personal goals possesses the characteristics listed below in Table 3.2.

SMART goals have five characteristics found in the letters that make up the word SMART.

Table 3.2. What are SMART goals?

Specific – you and your coach know exactly what the goal is.

Measurable – your progress toward the goal can be measured by yourself and others.

Attainable – you are able to make progress toward and attain the goal, and you believe that you can realize this outcome.

Relevant – by attaining the goal, you will have become a better tennis player; the goal is relevant to your development as a tennis player.

Timeframe – you have a clear idea and understanding of when you expect to attain the goal.

Following is a set of procedures that will show you how to make each personal goal a SMART goal and help you to enhance your commitment to it.

Procedures to set SMART Goals

Be specific.

1. SPECIFIC – Specify each goal.

Do this by placing each goal on a copy of the Personal Goals Form (Figure 3-2). A personal goal that is stated in a nonspecific way such as "I want to improve my backhand" or "I want to win more matches" does not convey enough information to you about precisely where you want to be or to go. Be specific in terms of the process of performing, actual performance, and your tennis development.

Specific goals convey specific information to both you and your coach.

Also, with the general kinds of goals as stated above, it is not clear what "improvement" or "winning" means.

Furthermore, it is difficult to know precisely what actions to take to attain the goals.

Be as specific as you can

In contrast, a personal goal such as "to improve my top-spin backhand down the line," or "to improve the percentage of my first serve" are more specific kinds of personal goals.

These goals convey more information to you about what you want to accomplish. They also provide this same information to your coach so that he/she knows how to proceed in order to help you attain these specific goals in terms of instruction and other personal actions.

The more specific you can make a personal goal, the greater the chance you will be motivated by it.

The more specific, the more motivated

The more specific you can make a personal goal—without being trivial—the greater the chance you will be motivated by it.

This is because it will be clearer and allow you to more

easily proceed toward your goal and monitor yourself during your progress. In turn, you will put more personal effort into practice and training to attain the goal.

Learn how to measure your goals so that you can better follow through with them.

2. MEASURABLE – Determine how to measure your progress.

Once your personal goals have been specified, you now need to accurately and actively measure your progress toward each goal. By doing this, you are more likely to remain focused on your goals and committed to the actions necessary to attain them.

Without measuring progress toward each of your personal goals, you are much more likely to lose interest in each one and not follow through on your actions.

Measure your progress on the rating scale

Measurement of progress toward each of your personal goals can occur by rating your progress toward it. You can do this by using the rating scale included on the Personal Goals Form (Figure 3-2) and by indicating a date when you will make these evaluations.

Using the rating scale, give yourself a numerical rating indicating the degree to which you believe you are making progress toward the goal.

Review your practice and match play performance.

Review your actual performance

In addition to this kind of rating, you can measure yourself by reviewing your actual performance—both during practice and match play—in relation to each of your goals.

If you have set a specific personal goal as discussed above, you will have included one or more performance indicators in the goal statement. Further, you can provide evaluation comments at the bottom of the Personal Goals Form.

Ask your coach to rate you

Make ratings to measure your progress not only by yourself but also ask your coach to make ratings for you. Then you can discuss your ratings in comparison to those made by your coach to determine the areas where your ratings are similar to or different from your coach's.

Compare your ratings with those of your coach. Determine where you may be similar or different.

We suggest that you make these ratings on a routine basis at least every two weeks. For your information, Figures 3-3 and 3-4, on pages 56 and 57, are illustrations of completed Personal Goals Forms with various kinds of sample goals and ratings.

3. ATTAINABLE – Make sure you can attain each goal.

If you have specified a personal goal, you should believe that you can attain it. If, however, you question your ability to attain the goal, you need to determine why you are in doubt and investigate what you can do to eliminate your doubt.

To make sure you can attain your personal goals, you should discuss each one of them with your coach. In this way, both of you can decide whether each goal is appropriate or if a more basic goal needs to be substituted for it.

Break down personal goals into simpler components if they become too complicated to accomplish.

Sometimes, a personal goal needs to be divided into more basic goals. For example, if you had a personal goal of being able to effectively return a spin serve to an 80 percent level of execution, you might find that you need to focus more on a goal of just getting the ball back into play rather than concentrating on a specific target. In this type of situation, a more basic goal needs to be attained first before you try to accomplish the other one.

Challenge yourself

If a personal goal that you have set seems to be an attainable one, but you still have doubts of whether you will be able to attain it, challenge yourself to pursue it. Look at yourself as objectively as possible.

When you know you possess the fundamental skills to make progress toward and attain a specific goal that you have set for yourself, make sure you know what actions to take to attain it (this will be discussed in the chapter on self-discipline).

Attaining your goals is dependent on knowing what actions to take.

Encourage yourself to trust yourself—let yourself go—and pursue the goal (this will be discussed further in the chapter on self-confidence).

4. RELEVANT – Know why each goal is relevant.

For each personal goal that you specify, make sure you know what it means with respect to your tennis performance. A relevant goal is one that, when attained, will make you a better tennis player. In addition, a relevant goal will be a source of self-motivation for you.

Know and determine why your goals are relevant.

To know how and why each one of your personal goals is relevant, ask and answer the following questions for yourself:

- ◆ If I attain the goal, how will it make me a better tennis player?
- ◆ If I do not attain this goal, will my tennis development be adversely affected?

5. TIMEFRAME – Consider a timeframe for goal attainment.

When you specify a personal goal, consider the amount of time that will be needed to attain it. Reaching your personal goals does not occur overnight. Anything worthwhile takes time. Therefore, when you know whether a goal is likely to be attained over a shorter or longer term, you can focus your attention and pace your activities accordingly.

Determine your goals in terms of short-term and long-term attainability.

You can make a determination about an appropriate timeframe for attainment of a goal by placing your goals into a logical order.

Some goals can be considered as short-term goals because they can be attained in a short period such as a week or a month. Other goals require more time. These can be referred to as long-term goals—ones that may require several months or even years to make substantial progress toward or to attain.

3. Discuss your goals with other people.

Once you have selected five to six important personal goals from your master list and placed these personal goals on a copy of the Personal Goals Form (Figure 3-2), it will be helpful to you to discuss these goals with other people such as your tennis coach, trainer, and parents.

Discussing your personal goals with other people will help you in several ways.

1 First, this will give you feedback from someone who may see a goal or area of your tennis performance that is important, but not necessarily reflected by your goals.

For example, your coach might observe that all of your personal goals focused on your groundstrokes from the baseline and that your volley, which is also important to your game as an all-court player, was not properly reflected by your goals.

Your coach will help you identify any gaps in your most important goals so that, if necessary, they can be changed.

2 A second reason for discussing your goals with other people is that you now have someone else who knows what you are working on, what you are working toward, why it is important to you, and the timeframe in which you expect to accomplish it. These individuals can give you feedback on their ratings of your progress toward your goals.

Involving other individuals in the evaluation of progress toward your goals will also help you sustain your commitment to your goals, particularly over the long range. Discussing your goals with other people is an efficient and effective way for you to take the lead to get them involved positively in your game. This process helps to make you a more mentally efficient tennis player.

Discussing your goals with other people is an efficient and effective way for you to take the lead to get them involved positively in your game.

Steps to discussing your goals with other people

In discussing your personal goals with other people, here are some steps you can take:

Step 1

Give the individual (e.g., your coach) a copy of your personal goals to review. On the copy, explain how you determined your goals on the master list and why you selected each.

Step 2

Ask the individual to make recommendations for other goals that are not on the copy you gave them, but that should have been included. If this person makes recommendations, ask them why so that you understand their reasoning.

Seek the help, guidance, and ongoing support and monitoring of others.

Step 3

Based on the discussion with the individual, make any changes on a copy of the Personal Goals Form and your master list of goals, as necessary.

Step 4

Ask the person to help you monitor your progress toward one or more of your goals.

4. Monitor the progress you make toward your goals.

To stay motivated, you need to know the amount of progress that you are making toward attainment of your personal goals and how quickly that progress is being

Figure 3-3. Personal Goals Form
Tennis Skills Goals Examples

Name: Jose Lambert   **Style of Play**: Serve and Volley

Date Goal Set: 3/25

Rating Scale
1 = Excellent

Evaluation Date: 4/25
2 = Good
3 = Average
4 = Fair
5 = Poor

Goals	Progress Rating
1. Improve B-H topspin down the line.	2
2. Improve B-H volley down the line.	3
3. Improve slice serve wide to deuce court.	2
4. Improve B-H slice approach shot.	1
5. Improve B-H topspin down the line passing shot.	5

Comments:

1. Need more practice on B-H passing shot accuracy.

2. Need more "punch" motion on down the line B-H volley.

Figure 3-4. Personal Goals Form
Strength and Conditioning Goals Examples

Name: Jose Lambert   **Style of Play**: Serve and Volley

Date Goal Set: 3/25

Evaluation Date: 4/25

Rating Scale
1 = Excellent
2 = Good
3 = Average
4 = Fair
5 = Poor

Goals	Progress Rating
1. I need to improve my quickness.	3
2. I need to strengthen my legs.	3
3. I need to strengthen my upper body.	4
4. I need to feel I can play a long match.	2
5. I need to improve my flexibility.	2
6. I need to improve my movement.	3

Comments:

1. I think I have improved my endurance and maintained my quickness.

2. I need more upper body strength.

achieved. This knowledge about your progress applies to all of your goals: tennis skills, physical fitness and condition, and your daily living skills.

If you do not know where you stand with respect to your personal goals and aspirations, it will be difficult for you to focus on what you have to do to realize these accomplishments and to sustain your follow-through. Consequently, you jeopardize losing focus, interest, and commitment because you will not know where you are in your progress now relative to where you have come from and where you are going.

The activity of monitoring your progress as a tennis player toward your personal goals and other relevant outcomes (e.g., performance in national or international play) will help keep you motivated and contribute to your mental efficiency. Toward that end, here are some ways to monitor your progress:

1. Know where you started.

To decide how much progress you have made toward a personal goal, you need to know where you began. That point in time is often referred to as a "benchmark," or point of reference.

If you have not established such a benchmark about your skill or performance, you will not be able to evaluate how much progress you have made.

How does a benchmark help?

For example, if you are aware of the fact that when you began your Mental Efficiency Program and daily tracking you were very inconsistent with your passing shots off the backhand side, you now have a benchmark to compare your progress.

Learn to monitor your progress on a continual basis.

Know where you started.

Establish a "benchmark" to know where you began and from which to measure your progress.

If you have already set SMART personal goals for yourself, such as we discussed in a previous section, you will have made yourself aware of where you began and what the goal is.

Know where you are now.

For other goals—like your performance in tournament play—you also will need to establish a benchmark point with regard to competition.

Once you know where you started and what the goal is, you can easily monitor your progress in a systematic and accurate way using the charts and forms of the Mental Efficiency Program.

2. Know where you are now.

Make ratings of the progress you are making toward each of your goals on a regular basis. In this way, you will know where you are at any particular point in time. Using your Personal Goals Form, you can actually make ratings as often as every week.

Determine your progress now for each of your goals.

For other goals, such as your progress in competitive match play during a season or semester, you can make judgments about your progress over longer periods of time (e.g., on a monthly or seasonal basis as matches occur). The important thing to do is to build into your schedule a system for determining where you are in the present in terms of your tennis development and performance.

Have planned discussions with your coach.

It is also very important to have planned discussions with your coach about your progress.

Knowing where you are now and where you came from will allow you to effectively measure your progress.

When you know where you are, then you are able to compare your current level against where you began.

When you determine that you are not making the progress that you expected, you now have a more factual basis for that evaluation rather than relying solely on your

Know where you are heading.

subjective opinion or that of others. You can then discuss these results with your coach and others and make any necessary adjustments in your training or competitive play.

When you do make the progress you expected, you can be proud of those results and take satisfaction in them.

3. Know where you are heading now.

Based on the progress you have made to date, you can now reaffirm to yourself that you are heading toward an attainable goal, or you can revise the goal as may be required. This reaffirmation or, if necessary, revision to one or more of your goals or aspirations helps you to continue to be motivated and assists you in getting back into a positive state.

Be flexible and able to adjust your goals based on your progress.

4. Know about your effort.

To make progress toward your personal goals, you must take particular actions and be able to follow through on them. Although this subject will be discussed in detail in the chapter of the book on self-discipline, part of monitoring your progress is determining both the quantity and quality of your effort.

Learn to define and monitor the quantity and the quality of your practice and progress. Quantity refers to the number of times you practice. Quality refers to the extent of effort you expend to achieve your goals.

Quantity and Quality

Quantity of effort defined in the context of mental efficiency means the number of times that you have practiced or worked out, and the frequency with which you have followed through on your plans and commitments.

By quality of effort, we are referring to the extent to which you went all out, gave your best effort, focused on attaining your goals, and did your best job.

You can monitor the quantity and quality of your effort in pursuing your goals by asking and answering the following questions:

◆ To what extent have I followed through to attain each of my goals?

◆ To what degree have I focused my attention and time on attaining each of my goals?

In answering each of these questions, you can rate yourself as follows:

1 = Excellent
2 = Good
3 = Average
4 = Fair
5 = Poor

Make these types of ratings on a daily basis or every time that you work toward your goals. Based on these ratings, you might decide that changes are necessary in your goals, plans, actions, or quality of effort. These kinds of changes typically are expected and characteristic of the mentally efficient tennis player.

Making changes in your goals is characteristic of the mentally efficient tennis player.

5. Use visualization.

Visualization can be used as a means to enhance your self-motivation. Visualization is a personal process that involves the forming of mental images, or pictures, about your tennis performance. Visualization is also referred to as mental imagery.

When you visualize yourself doing something well, you are also helping to increase your desire to perform that way and to take the necessary actions.

Research on athletes and other kinds of performers, including tennis players, suggests that visualization serves performance enhancement purposes.

Visualization is a personal process that involves the forming of mental images, or pictures, about your tennis performance.

Picture Yourself Succeeding

A visual image is the basis of the process of visualization.

In this regard, a visual image is a picture of yourself performing at a peak level as a tennis player. You can also visualize someone else in their performance.

For example, when you think about—and see—yourself hitting the "perfect" lob on an important game point, you are using the process of visualization. When you visualize someone else doing this, you are also using the process.

Watch a videotape

You are also using visualization when you watch a videotape of yourself playing tennis. For example, viewing yourself on a video executing a stroke that had given you trouble during match play will help you become more confident in this shot's execution the next time you are confronted with it in a match situation.

The more often you use the process of visualization, the better your chances are of being motivated to hit and execute the specific shot. Through use of visualization, you can put yourself in positive states of thought and emotion.

You visualize first by watching an actual image on the videotape and then you go about seeing that image again and again in your "mind's eye." Make sure that this actual image and your mental image of it are technically correct.

You can use visual or mental images to help you become and remain motivated at different times and in various situations. These include use of visualization to help you in training, during match warmup, during changeovers, to remain in a positive state before serving, prior to studying school subjects, taking school exams, and at other times.

You can form pictures of yourself playing tennis by using videotapes and also through looking at still photographs. You also can watch the top professional players during competition and visualize yourself doing the same things that they do in similar situations.

Through use of visualization—in all the examples given above—you can put yourself in positive states of thought and emotion. In doing so, these positive states will help you want to do what it takes to perform well on the court.

Listed below are steps that you can follow that will help you create positive mental images effectively and use the process of visualization.

Step 1

Create meaningful images.

Identify the types of mental images that are meaningful to you, given your level of development as a tennis player and your style of play. For example, if you are primarily a serve and volley type player, you might want to develop a more penetrating backhand volley.

By creating a meaningful image of yourself hitting a forceful and deep backhand volley in a variety of point situations, you are able to develop a mental image—one in which you can even feel and see yourself execute the shot, create feelings of confidence, hear the sound of the ball and the cheer of the crowd, and actually "participate" in the image experience.

Make the mental images relate to your goals.

Step 2

Make sure that each mental image you identify relates to one of your important personal goals. Further, try to make each mental image one in which you are executing in a technically correct way, where the results of your efforts are in your favor, and where you feel energized or positive by the image.

Step 3

Make a list of your personal goals and the associated mental images. Describe the images on the Positive Images Form.

Make a list of several mental images that have to do with your personal goals and that are "right for you." You should develop at least one image per goal.

Step 4

You can describe these mental images on the Positive Images Form, seen in Figures 3-5 and 3-6 on pages 66 and 67. As you will note, Figure 3-6 is filled in as an actual example.

Step 5

You have identified and described the important mental images that can help put you in a motivated state. Following this, you can now determine the situations and times that are best for you to use these mental images as part of the visualization process.

Visualization should be scheduled and not random.

It is important to pinpoint precise times for visualization. Visualization is more effective when it is scheduled and not random. By scheduling your visualization, the success of this procedure will be greatly increased.

Please note the situations and times when you will be using your mental images in the space provided on the Positive Images Form.

Step 6

Using the times you have listed on the Positive Images Form, engage in the actual process of visualizing yourself in the ways that you have described.

As you visualize, try to see yourself as clearly and vividly as possible—if possible even in color—and "feel" the positive sensations associated with yourself performing at a high level of achievement.

Collect visual images of yourself that you can refer to often for reference and reinforcement.

You will experience feelings of confidence, desire, assertiveness, or being in control. Put yourself as much as possible into a "real" state and situation through vivid imagery and feelings.

Step 7

In addition to the above mental imagery procedure, you are also encouraged to gather photographs or videotapes of yourself performing in positive ways on the tennis court. You can keep these still pictures in a scrapbook and perhaps produce a motivational videotape library for yourself.

Step 8

Look at the still pictures and your videos. When you do so, try to experience the same positive feelings that you had when you created mental images. In fact, you can use these pictures and videos as a springboard for a mental imagery session.

Step 9

Look at the still pictures and your videos on a regularly scheduled basis.

Remind yourself to be sure that you are engaging in visualization, picture watching, and video viewing for about 10-15 minutes at a time. This may be done every day, or every other day, or as indicated on the Positive Images Form (Figure 3-5).

Step 10

Evaluate the effectiveness of how you are using visualization by discussing with your coach how you are doing. Make any changes in the procedure that you are using as might be required. Make sure to continue to add to your positive images throughout the tennis season.

Add to your positive images throughout the tennis season.

6. Use positive affirmations.

An affirmation is a statement that you make about some aspect of your performance as a tennis player. A positive affirmation is a positive statement that you make about your performance. This can also be referred to as positive self-talk.

You should use positive affirmations to help put yourself into an effective mental, emotional, and physical state. When you are in this kind of positive state, your motivation will be high both as a player and as a person. This will keep your mental efficiency at a very high level.

Positive affirmations will help maintain your motivation.

Use of positive affirmations will help you focus and concentrate on what you are trying to accomplish on the court and to reestablish your focus after you lose it.

Here are examples of positive affirmations made by tennis

Figure 3-5. Positive Images Form

Name: **Date:**

Style of Play:

Images: PSAC-Championship Finals

1. I toss the ball perfectly into the court I jump into it and serve wide bringing him off the court. He hits a weak shot which I hit with a bh volley crosscourt for a winner

2. The next point I serve right down the T. He hits an awkward pop up shot. I run in change to a semi western grip and punish it for a FH winner

3. I see myself returning a ad court serve wide with a beautiful BH cross court clipping the line

4. I see myself in a rally I hit a FH down the line which he returns CC which I hit a bh shot down the line with topspin for a winner

5. I see myself returning a wide serve deuce court with a beautiful FH crosscourt pulling him off the baseline. He hits the ball to the ad court wide I run around my backhand for an inside-out FH

6. I see myself in a long rally in a tie-breaker no 9-10 match point I am running down every ball, I hit a bh slice approach which he hits to my FH side I lunge beautifully hitting it crosscourt for a winner.

7. I see match point I serve down the T deuce court he hits a lob as I come to the net. I launch myself into it to hit an overhead for a winner and the championship

Situations and times when I will use these images:

1. Thirty minutes before I play
2. Before I go to bed
3. On changeovers
4. When I awake in the morning

Figure 3-6. Sample Positive Images Form

Name: Judy Lansing   **Date**: 7/30

Style of Play: Serve and volley

Images:
1. I serve wide in the deuce court, pull my opponent out of position, and then volley crosscourt for the winner.

2. I hit the ball very well crosscourt and love to run my opponent from side to side until they make an error.

3. I see myself on the stadium court at Wimbledon – in the championship match – serving for matchpoint.

4. I see myself as Steffi Graf running side to side punishing the ball flat and deep to each corner unmercifully.

5. I see myself as Chris Evert holding the trophy at Wimbledon.

Situations and times when I will use these images:

1. Thirty minutes before I play.

2. At 8:00 every evening after dinner.

3. On changeovers in my matches.

4. When I awake in the morning I feel alert and confident.

players to help themselves be motivated:

◆ I am hitting through the ball very well.

◆ I feel in total harmony on the court.

◆ I am aggressive yet controlled.

◆ My court movement is very fluid.

◆ I feel light on my feet.

◆ I know I'm going to win.

◆ Everything I hit works for me.

Use of positive affirmations will help you focus and concentrate on what you are trying to accomplish on the court and to reestablish your focus after you lose it.

Features of affirmations

Affirmations have many common features. These may include:

◆ Each phrase is stated in the present tense, as if it were happening at the moment, not in the future.

◆ Each statement is positive and identifies an accomplishment or condition.

◆ Each statement is communicated to yourself quietly—in what is called subvocal speech.

Here are some steps to follow that will help you formulate and use positive affirmations to support your self-motivation:

Step 1

Identify the specific and positive states that you want to possess as a tennis player.

Identify the specific and positive states that you want to possess as a tennis player. These qualities may have to do with mental and physical tennis skills, aspects of physical fitness and condition, or daily living skills. The following are examples of such specific and positive states:

• Focusing on the ball before impact.

• Keeping my hands relaxed to accelerate through the ball when I hit it.

• Feeling confident throughout each game, set, and match.

• Staying composed even when struggling against a tough opponent.

Step 2

You can develop a master list of the specific and positive states that you want to possess. In developing this list, first write down all of the possibilities before selecting particular ones on which to focus your attention.

Step 3

Select from your master list of specific and positive states, five or six of the most important ones. These should be ones that relate to your personal goals and outcomes.

Write a positive affirmation for each specific and positive state.

Step 4

For each of the positive and specific states that you have selected, write a positive affirmation. You can then place these statements on a copy of the Positive Affirmations Form, Figure 3-7, on page 70. A sample of this form is seen as Figure 3-8.

Step 5

In relation to the positive affirmations, write down on the form the exact situations and times that you expect to use these statements.

Examples are when you lose focus on the court; when you are warming up before a match; or between glances at others during match play.

Step 6

Use the positive affirmations with the flexibility to make changes in them, based on how they are valuable to your performance.

Figure 3-7. Positive Affirmations Form

Name: **Date:**

Style of Play:

Positive States	**Positive Affirmations**
1. I have quick feet	1. I am always on my toe
2. I am phsically fit	2. I can compete all day I never will give up
3. I have patience on my serve	3. I am always going to get my serve in
4. I focus on the ball before impact	4. I am always focused in every shot
5. I can create shots and hit winners	5. I am always ready to hit a winner at anytime
6. I always hit the ball out and in front	6. I have good reflexes
7. I will remain poised no matter what	7. I will always move on to the next point, not lose concentration

Situations and times when I will use these affirmations:

1. During warm-up
2. When I wake up everyday
3. Thirty minutes before I play
4. During times when things are not going well
5. At night before I go to bed

Figure 3-8. Sample Positive Affirmations Form

Name: Silvia Ramirez   Date: 11/19

Style of Play: Serve and volley

Positive States

1. I have quick feet.

2. I have good balance.

3. I have patience at the baseline.

4. I am physically fit.

5. I am very steady.

Positive Affirmations

1. I am very light on my feet.

2. I feel very surefooted today.

3. I'm not going to miss no matter what.

4. I feel like I can compete all day.

5. Everything I hit works.

Situations and times when I will use these affirmations:

1. One hour at night alone in my room (8:00 p.m.).

2. Thirty minutes before my match starts.

3. During warmup.

4. When I wake up on match day.

5. When I look at the draw.

CHAPTER SUMMARY

In this chapter, we have focused on self-motivation as a quality of the mentally efficient tennis player. We have discussed the need for a player to become and remain motivated both in terms of the personal benefits that can be derived as well as the problems that can be prevented by being self-motivated.

We then discussed Step 2 of the Mental Efficiency Program: Know what you want to accomplish and why.

This chapter outlined what to do and how to proceed in order to help build your self-motivation:

◆ Identify personal goals for yourself.

◆ Make a commitment to your goals.

◆ Discuss your goals with other people.

◆ Monitor the progress you make toward your goals.

◆ Use visualization.

◆ Use positive affirmations.

We now are ready to discuss the next area of mental efficiency, that of self-confidence.

4

BUILDING AND MAINTAINING SELF-CONFIDENCE

Jim Courier at the U.S. Open.

Never, never, never quit.
Winston Churchill
British Statesman

My mother taught me very early to believe I could achieve any accomplishment I wanted. The first was to walk without braces."
Wilma Rudolph
1960 Olympian

I just play with what I have left.
Pancho Gonzalez
Tennis Player

Man is what he believes.
Anton Chekhov
Russian Writer

Years after Jim Courier had left the Academy and won his first Grand Slam, he looked back and described being at the NBTA for the first time as one of his most frightening experiences. He was away from home, friends, and family, still wondering if tennis (and not baseball) was really the right sport; and with a group of players and talent that would scare anyone—even today—Agassi, Wheaton, Knowles, D. Flach, Kass, Navarez, Garner, and Caswell.

Courier was not flamboyant like Agassi. He was the work horse and carried the heavy load on his back in school and on the court. He made every decision a struggle. Whether or not he would go to college—as opposed to playing the circuit right away—was a major decision for Jim and his family and one of the most important they ever made.

At about this time, we had the NBTA Traveling Team in place, initially coached by my son Jimmy. The thought was to play on the circuit with other NBTA hopefuls and not accept the prize money past qualified expenses so as to protect college (and scholarship) opportunities. The Team was a huge success and produced some of the top players in the game today. It also gave those participating a chance to see what life was really like on the road and a taste of whether they wanted it badly enough and whether they felt they had a chance to make it.

After this experience, Courier never looked back. As with all of his decisions, he reached down deep within himself, did his research, tested his options, and then moved forward.

Interestingly, as Jim began his ascent to the top, I was also forced to make a decision that was critical to both our careers. At the time, I had Seles, Agassi, and Wheaton as well as Courier (the right kind of problem to have, I guess, as I entered my fourth decade in the game and my seventh in life). I, and they, knew that I could not do justice to them all as their coach and a hard choice had to be made. It was the most difficult

and agonizing decision I have ever had to make in my whole life. It was like having to choose which of your three children could live and which had to die.

I chose Agassi. He was like a son to me. I will never regret that decision. He is a close friend and I hope always will be. He needed me, and he has done well. I know that I made the right choice, and I will never look back.

Jim decided to go with Hiqueras and has reached the top. Jim and I talk often. He is one of my son's best friends. We reflect often on the days in which the decision was made. He says that the time he spent at the Academy with me made it possible for him to be where he is today. What a great tribute from such a fine young man.

I know that in the beginning, he was resentful and wanted to "get back" at me for my choice. When he played Agassi, it was a vendetta against both Andre and Nick. In his eyes he was saying to us, "I'm going to stick it to you." And he did! And do you know what, Jim? I'm glad and very happy for you. You deserve it, and I will always look back with pride on our time together and what you have done. You believed in yourself and in your ability, and you have done it all. God bless you, Jim Courier.

Nick Bollettieri

changes on the tennis court and in other areas of your life as you grow. When you are self-confident, your chances of being a mentally efficient tennis player are greatly increased.

For example, you may not have the skills at the moment to compete at a national level of tournament play. But if you believe that you can make progress toward that goal, and you participate in regular planned practices, training, and proper skills execution, you are moving forward with self-confidence.

NOT FOR TENNIS ONLY...

The same holds true for other areas of your life such as school. You may be enrolled in a difficult academic course, but you believe that you can study effectively, learn to understand and master the material, and get a good grade. This belief in your capability and your taking action by mapping out a systematic study schedule reflect your self-confidence.

MAINTAIN POISE AND PERSEVERANCE

With self-confidence, you are able to maintain your poise and perseverance — two important indicators of a self-confident state.

With self-confidence, you are able to maintain your poise and perseverance—two important indicators of a self-confident state.

Poise is the ability to prevent getting upset with yourself or with the things going on around you.

Poise is your ability to prevent getting upset with yourself (e.g., losing a close match or hitting the wrong shot at the wrong time) and with things going on around you (e.g., calls from your opponent line judge, the wind, the sun), especially in competitive situations.

For example, if you are not doing well against an opponent during a crucial part of a set, you are poised if you do not get anxious or frustrated and can remain calm and relaxed. You are poised when you can focus on what is going on around you and remain as factual as possible—you don't get swept up by the emotion of the moment.

Perseverance means the extent to which you can follow

4 | BUILDING AND MAINTAINING SELF-CONFIDENCE

In this chapter, we discuss how you can build and maintain your self-confidence both as a tennis player and for life in general.

WHAT'S IN THIS CHAPTER

In this chapter, we discuss how you can build and maintain your self-confidence both as a tennis player and for life in general.

We provide you with guidelines, steps, and activities that will help you evaluate all the situations that you might realistically encounter and provide you with suggestions as to how you can best be prepared for them.

You will also learn how the systematic use of your senses—seeing, hearing, and feeling—can enhance the confidence you have about yourself and enable you to enjoy what you are doing, regardless of the obstacles involved.

When you are self-confident, you believe in your ability to follow through and to accomplish the goals that you have set for yourself.

WHY YOU NEED SELF-CONFIDENCE

When you are self-confident, you believe in your ability to follow through and to accomplish the goals you have set for yourself. This belief involves viewing positively how you do things—such as hitting a "kick" serve, practicing effectively, making progress over the long term to the next level, accepting constructive feedback on a daily basis, and making through on what you intended to do, especially in those competitive situations when you are not doing as well as you would have expected.

For example, there will be times in competitive tennis when you will be losing to an opponent because you are not playing well. Yet, despite your poor play, your desire to win and your effort to not give up allow you to stay calm, put aside negative thoughts and feelings, and regain the belief that you can do well in spite of it all.

BELIEVE IN YOURSELF

When you believe that you are able to compete on the tennis court with players of your ability level or better, your self-confidence promotes and sustains your performance. This will happen even though you may not be the most talented player or the best athlete.

Alternatively, if you do not believe in yourself and how you play the game, cannot rebound from poor play, cannot handle losing, and have negative thoughts about yourself and your tennis, you are probably defeated before you even begin the match.

GAIN PERSONAL BENEFITS

There are several benefits that you can gain by building and maintaining your self-confidence.

1 The first benefit is being able to trust yourself. Personal trust means feeling secure that you will do a quality job on the court whether it is during training or match play competition. You will be able to keep the trust that you have in yourself even though the result of a game, set, or match does not go in your favor.

Many times, your performance will not meet your expectations. This is not necessarily negative. Personal trust means that you believe that you will make the necessary adjustments

Perseverance means being able to follow through with your plans no matter what the obstacles.

When you believe that you are able to compete on the tennis court with players of your ability level or better, your self-confidence promotes and sustains your performance.

Trust yourself.

to your game so you can continue to get better.

In terms of mental efficiency, personal trust involves letting yourself go and not worrying about what you are doing. Your concentration should be on performing and not overthinking or analyzing. Playing tennis in this way allows you to enjoy the process and challenge of competition.

Have faith in your training and ability.

2 A second personal benefit that has to do with self-confidence is the belief—or expectancy—that you will be able to prepare successfully for your next match or event, follow through, and not let yourself down. You believe that you can and will make the necessary adjustments in your technique, mental approach, or game strategy to accomplish what you set out to do.

This is the case during any pressure situation, either on or off the tennis court.

Balancing the mental and physical aspects of tennis allows you to reach your potential.

3 A third personal benefit that relates to self-confidence and your mental efficiency has to do with your ability to easily stay in personal balance. This means coordinating positive thoughts and images about yourself, with effective management of your emotions, coupled with smooth physical actions such as execution of effective groundstrokes.

Balancing the mental and physical aspects of tennis allows you to reach your potential.

PREVENT PROBLEMS

By being self-confident, you prevent several problems from occurring.

1 First, you effectively eliminate feelings of fear and failure. Since you believe in yourself and your abilities, you can recover yourself mentally and emotionally from the loss of a match and get right back into training for the next competition.

2 Second, you are able to eliminate any perceptions that you might have of yourself as being inadequate. You can determine areas of skills and techniques in your game that need improvement. You will recognize these temporary limitations and maintain confidence without diminishing your belief and expectation of yourself with regard to your long-term goals.

Believing in yourself helps to eliminate inadequate self-perceptions and feelings of failure, fear, and intimidation.

3 Third, you refuse to be intimidated by an opponent's performance, behavior, or gamesmanship tactics on—or off—the court.

Step 3

Build and maintain confidence in yourself.

By taking this step and by being committed to it, you can increase your chances of being a self-confident tennis player and person. We encourage you to undertake several confidence building and maintenance activities.

You should engage in these activities on a regular and consistent basis. They are listed below:

Practice building and maintaining your self-confidence on a regular basis.

1. Establish an agreement with yourself.

2. Assess your self-confidence.

3. Know your current level of skill.

4. Appraise your situation and results realistically.

5. Monitor your senses.

6. Use breathing to your advantage.

7. Learn to relax.

8. Use thought control.

Each activity is more fully discussed in the remainder of this chapter.

1. Establish an agreement with yourself.

Building and maintaining your self-confidence is not only an important step to take in being a mentally efficient tennis player and individual, but it is also a challenging task.

It is challenging because tennis is an intricate, highly skilled, and fast-paced, exciting sport. Self-confidence is a personal quality that is not easily learned or improved upon without experience and practice. One must not lose perspective of this reality and develop negative thinking or experience emotions that create a nonconfident state. This is especially likely to happen during competitive situations.

Agree to make personal commitments

To prevent a loss of self-confidence and to be able to create a situation so that you can focus on confident thoughts, feelings, and actions, we suggest that you come to a personal agreement with yourself. This agreement will include several personal commitments relating to self-confidence, as described below.

You will not doubt yourself

You will not doubt yourself. Remember that doubt, worry, and fear are not real—they are created by your thoughts and feelings. To set the conditions to dispel these thoughts, emotions, and negative states, you must commit to doing a quality job in all areas of mental efficiency—personal awareness, motivating yourself, self-discipline, and all other areas.

Give your best

You will give your best to improve your game. You will do this by not "selling yourself short." You will give each practice session, point, and game your full and undivided attention and effort. In doing so, you play each point—in practice or competition—with the same effort and concentration.

Make a personal commitment with yourself.

Do not doubt yourself or your ability.

Strive to improve and play your best.

You are not perfect

You will agree that you are not perfect and that trying to be perfect is not realistic or helpful to you or your tennis. It is helpful to you, however, to recognize that you can learn from your mistakes and use them as a basis for your development—both on and off the court.

Be realistic – you cannot be perfect.

Trust yourself

You will trust yourself to play each point of every game with total effort yet in a relaxed manner—enjoying the process.

Trust yourself and your capabilities.

Expect to be your best every time

You will anticipate and expect to perform well every time you play—in practice or competition. Expect to be your best every time you play.

View events as positive challenges

You will view pressure situations and quality opponents as positive challenges that make tennis fun and worthwhile—challenging you to be your best.

Challenge yourself to reach your very best.

Maintain your worth as a person

You will not equate your performance as a tennis player with your worth as a person.

Write yourself a letter

You may want to add additional points to the personal commitments you make with yourself. In fact, you may want to write these commitments down in a letter to yourself. This will serve as a reminder to you that having self-confidence starts with an agreement that you want to become and remain confident in what you do and who you are on a consistent basis.

Separate your performance in sport from your self-worth in life.

2. Assess your self-confidence.

To build and maintain your self-confidence, it is helpful to determine your current level of confidence in various aspects of your tennis and your life. By knowing your self-confidence level, two positive actions should result for you.

Determine your own level of self-confidence.

1 First, you will be more inclined to take some personal action aimed at improving your self-confidence simply by going through the process of self-assessment.

2 Second, you will come to recognize and appreciate that there are many dimensions to self-confidence and that self-confidence is within your reach with a limited amount of effort and commitment on your part.

There are several easy-to-identify indicators that you can use to help determine whether you are improving (or not) in building your self-confidence levels.

Below are some procedures to follow that will help you assess your self-confidence in the sport of tennis, which, in turn, contributes to your mental efficiency.

Quality indicators of self-confidence

Believe in the fact that you have the skills necessary to perform well – or if you don't – you will be able to develop them within your training program.

Recognize that self-confidence is not a "thing" or "state of mind" that is out there to be obtained. Rather, it is important to understand that self-confidence actually involves many different dimensions—each of which is a quality indicator of self-confidence.

By knowing what these indicators are, you can assess your self-confidence. The self-confidence quality indicators are listed below.

◆ Believe that you possess the required skills—tennis and life—necessary to perform well. Skills you don't currently have you will develop.

◆ Understand that during any performance or competition, you will need to make changes and adjustments in how you play (sport is dynamic; nothing remains the same; change is expected).

◆ Make an agreement with yourself that you will make every effort to learn new skills, refine existing ones, and make necessary adjustments in how you play.

When are you confident?

With the above quality indicators in mind, determine the conditions and situations where you are confident in relation to your tennis. Toward this end, you can ask yourself the following questions:

◆ What are the times when I consider myself to be in a confident state: during practice; prematch warmup; match play; other times?

◆ What aspects of my game are the ones in which I am most confident: baseline play; midcourt play; net play; mental approach; serve; other aspects?

◆ What is it that makes me confident in the above situations and aspects of my game: what I think; what I say; how I feel; skill level; preparation; other?

Use the Tennis Self-Confidence Survey

Once you have considered and responded to these questions, you can now record information on the Tennis Self-Confidence Survey (Figure 4-1) in the spaces provided. By doing so, you will have a clear idea of what times and in which areas you are self-confident.

When are you not confident?

Ask yourself several questions that have to do with the times and conditions when you are not confident about your tennis. In this regard, consider these questions:

◆ What are the times when I consider myself not to be in a confident state: during practice; prematch warmup; match play; other times?

Sport is dynamic. You will have to continually change, learn, and refine during your development.

Determine when you ARE and when you ARE NOT confident.

Figure 4-1. Tennis Self-Confidence Survey

Name *Jack Gottlieb*   Date *4/11/97*

1. What are the times when I am usually in a confident state (e.g., during practice, prematch warmup, match play, other)?

   Usually during practice and match play

2. What aspects of my game are the ones in which I am usually confident (e.g., baseline play; midcourt play; net play; mental approach; serve; other)?

   Baseline play, midcourt play and serve

3. What is it that makes me confident?

   The way I feel, preparation being the key

4. What are the times when I am not confident?

   When things go wrong on particular shots. Not enough experience being the main reason for that. Not confident in my skills

5. What aspects of my game are ones in which I am not confident?

   Net play, backhand, approach shot (bh side)

6. What is it that does not make me confident?

   Lack of experience, still growing, An overwhelming desire and knowledge that I can be better w/proper facilities

◆ What aspects of my game are the ones in which I am least confident: baseline play; midcourt play; net play; mental approach; serve; other aspects?

◆ What is it that makes me least confident in the above situation and aspects of my game: what I think; what I say; how I feel; lack of skill; poor preparation; other?

You can also record your responses to the above questions on the Tennis Self-Confidence Survey (Figure 4-1).

What makes you confident?

The information that you have established about your self-confidence and recorded on the survey form can now be analyzed. This analysis can be accomplished by considering what factors are at work in helping you to be confident. Important factors are listed below. Determine which ones help you to be more confident.

◆ Your current skill development is equivalent to your level of play; you have worked at developing your skills.

◆ You have a sound way of preparing for matches and competitive events; this includes having quality practice and training sessions.

◆ You have personal goals that are specific, measurable, attainable, relevant, and timeframed.

◆ You are able to visualize yourself and talk to yourself in positive ways.

◆ Other factors.

What makes you lack confidence?

Just as you were able to determine what made you confident, it is also important to determine what factors make you lack confidence. These may be:

◆ You have not adequately developed some of your skills to a required level that allows you to perform well.

Determine which factors help you to be more confident.

It is important to determine what factors make you not confident.

◆ You do not have a consistent, effective, established method for training and preparing for competition.

◆ You do not have clearly stated personal goals that are important to you.

◆ You visualize yourself and talk to yourself in negative ways.

◆ Other factors.

Determine and know your current skills.

If you have conducted a thorough assessment of your self-confidence by way of the methods described above, you can now use this information during the self-confidence building activities to be discussed in the remainder of this chapter.

3. Know your current level of skill.

One factor that is very important to your self-confidence and mental efficiency is determining as accurately as possible your current level of skill development. This refers to your tennis skills, both physical and mental, as well as skills for effective daily living (e.g., general life skills—getting along with other people, study skills).

Skills are essential to your self-confidence because if you do not possess certain skills, it is very difficult for you to perform well on the tennis court and elsewhere.

Skills have to be maintained by consistent and quality practice habits.

If you do not have the skills necessary for success in what you are doing, your confidence is likely to be diminished—unless you have a plan to acquire and develop the skills you need (to be discussed in the chapter on self-discipline).

Skills in this context are not to be equated with the natural physical talent you were born with (such as your natural ability to run and jump). Tennis skills and skills for daily living are skills that can be acquired and developed through a sound plan and maintained by effective and efficient training and practice.

Maintain your skill levels

Here are some ways to keep up to date on your current level of skill development:

Conduct a routine inventory of your skills.

Conduct a routine inventory

Conduct a routine inventory of your skills. Forms to use to do this are the Tennis Skills Inventory (Figure 2-1), the Physical Fitness and Condition Rating Scale (Figure 2-2), and the Daily Living Skills Checklist (Figure 2-3). These forms are found in Chapter 2.

If you have conducted a thorough self-assessment, then using these instruments will help you be more knowledgeable about your skills. If not, we encourage you to fill out the forms now.

Get opinions from others who are interested in your development.

Obtain opinions and feedback

Obtain opinions and feedback about your skills from your coaches and other people who want to help you in tennis and life and who can provide you with objective information.

Determine your skills

Make sure you determine the skills that you have already developed to a good level. In this way, you can continue to practice and improve upon them in order to remain skilled. Specify the skills that need improvement.

Check your opponent's level

Examine your skill levels.

Make sure that you are practicing and competing against opponents at similar or higher skill levels. These decisions should be made in conjunction with your coach.

Your aim is to be successful at playing, while challenging yourself in a systematic way against better and better opponents with different skills and techniques.

4. Appraise your situations and results realistically.

For every situation you experience as a tennis player, you have an option as to how you react and analyze the result and outcome.

For example, you may be losing to an opponent whom you believe you are "supposed to beat" because you have more natural talent and existing skills. In this case, there are many ways you can appraise the situation.

Appraise your situations and results realistically.

You can view it in a negative way whereby you might tell yourself that you shouldn't be losing because you are the better player.

Or, you can view the situation as a challenge, determine how you can prove that you are indeed the better player, and refocus your game and efforts to win.

Off the tennis court suppose you have done poorly on a test, and now you have to decide whether you will spend more time studying for the next test or give up and settle for a low grade in the course. Here, too, you can view the situation in a negative or a positive way.

Positive vs. negative

It is up to you alone to determine how you react and view a particular situation.

How well you appraise all of your tennis situations—both on and off the court—can have a major effect on your self-confidence.

You have the option of deciding how you want to interpret events and situations in your life. You have the control of yourself to do so.

You can look at something that has happened to you realistically, according to the facts, and use that personal analysis in a positive way. If you have performed poorly in a match, for instance, you can face that fact and decide to use the match as a learning experience for your development.

On the other hand, you can view a personal experience by

You alone have the control to interpret situations and events in your life in a positive or negative manner.

not facing the facts, seeking excuses, and attributing the reasons for the situation to causes outside of yourself. If the facts are that you lost a match and that you performed poorly, you can decide to ignore the situation—running from reality—and justify it by pointing to things like the court surface, weather, or a judge. If you choose the more realistic "face-the-facts" positive option, you will feel good about yourself in spite of the setback, and your self-confidence will grow and develop. If you ignore the facts and do not face reality, your self-confidence is likely to diminish.

Make the positive, factual choice

When you encounter a situation that does not meet your expectations or results in a situation contrary to you, make sure you understand that the easy approach is to view the event negatively and to talk to yourself about it in a negative way. This results in undermining your self-confidence.

It can, however, be just as easy—although perhaps difficult the first few times that you try it, to view such situations in a factual way and as a springboard for your development and mental efficiency. Following are some suggestions for you:

No one is perfect

No one is perfect. Those who believe they are approach life unrealistically and set themselves up to fail.

Remind yourself that no individual is perfect at anything they do. This includes world class tennis players, other elite professional athletes, and you. No one is perfect. Those who believe they are approach life unrealistically and set themselves up to fail.

When somebody thinks about being perfect, they have immediately set themselves up to fail because the condition of perfectionism is factually impossible.

No matter how skilled someone is, there will always be some variation in how they execute a skill; their performance will vary from day to day. The task, therefore, is not to be perfect, but to do a quality job as consistently as possible and to be able to recognize and learn from things that did not happen as you expected.

Acknowledge the mistake

The first step to building self-confidence is acknowledging your mistakes.

When you know you have made a physical mistake or a mental error while playing tennis, it is important for your self-confidence that you acknowledge that fact. It is also important that you do something right away to minimize the mistake from occurring in the future.

A physical mistake has to do with factors like using an improper technique or being in the wrong position on the court.

A mental mistake has to do with factors like not remembering to keep your poise or not focusing on each serve.

Try to reduce the number of times the mistake occurs in the future.

When these kinds of mistakes happen, first acknowledge the mistake. Then, ask yourself what you did wrong and how you can learn from the situation so that you don't do it again. If you need to, ask for advice. Many times, it is difficult to recognize your own mistakes and limitations.

Decide what actions you can take to make sure you reduce the number of times that the mistake will occur in the future. These actions may have to do with acquiring more information about correct technique, varying your training, training harder, applying new procedures, or more skill work.

Don't blame others

Don't be adversely affected by things outside of your control. Focus on what you can control.

Do not blame your poor performance on things that are outside of yourself. Some external circumstances that can affect your performance are the weather, the quality or type of playing surface, presumed cheating by the opponent, parental pressure, or your physical condition. It is very difficult, if not impossible, to really do anything about these kind of things. And the harder you try, the more adversely they can affect you.

It is a more effective and efficient use of your time and energy to focus on things that you can do to improve your performance: (a) how you think about playing tennis, (b) how you feel when you play, and (c) skills, habits, and attitudes you can develop that will allow you to reach your best performance level.

Making every situation in tennis and life a learning experience is a healthy and positive way to approach sport and life.

Each activity is a learning experience

Consider each time you set foot on the tennis court as a learning experience. This includes training and competitive play. A learning experience is accepting reality—the facts about what you are doing—and then deciding what you have gained from that experience—good or bad—that will allow you to take actions to make you a better player and person. In this respect, we encourage you to spend some time after each practice session or match alone, and also with your coach, thinking about and discussing what you have learned and what you can do better during your next performance.

This kind of approval will boost your self-confidence because you are "taking charge" or control of things that you can do to shape your progress and performance. In essence, you are being mentally efficient at your tennis.

Put a particular situation into a fuller context to gain proper perspective.

What's the worst that can happen?

Take the personal position that when things do not go your way—either on or off the court—you will approach the situation or result straightforward and not avoid it. Ask yourself, "What would be the worst thing that could happen if I do not perform as expected in a given situation?" Weigh the importance of this one event against other factors in your life such as health, family, and your beliefs.

When you put into a fuller context a particular situation, chances are you will be able to place it in its proper perspective and remain confident about your next challenge.

You're in control

Don't ever forget that you alone have the ability to control how you think, feel, and act. You alone can decide to become and remain confident or to tell yourself you cannot be that way. We encourage you to make the decision to become and remain self-confident by realistically facing your situations and challenges—both on and off the tennis court.

5. Monitor your senses.

It will be helpful in the development of your self-confidence as well as your overall mental efficiency for you to be aware of your senses—especially under competitive conditions such as match play. When you are aware of your senses and can monitor them, you can take action to change things that are limiting your self-confidence. You can also build on the positive things that are happening to you.

Three particular senses are important for you to be aware of and to monitor. These senses are referred to as your visual sense, auditory sense, and kinesthetic sense.

Visual sense refers to the things that you see while playing (e.g., the movements of your opponent) and the things you are imagining about yourself while performing (mental imagery).

Auditory sense reflects the sounds that you hear while playing (e.g., sounds of the crowd, referee's call) as well as the things you say to yourself (e.g., positive or negative self-talk).

Kinesthetic sense really means the muscular sensations (e.g., looseness, tightness) you experience as you play tennis.

Inhibitors vs. enhancers

When you monitor your visual, auditory, and kinesthetic senses, you become more aware of things that are likely to either inhibit or enhance your self-confidence. The inhibitors and enhancers of self-confidence have to do with:

You alone are in control of your ability to be (or not be) self-confident.

Learn to recognize and monitor three important senses: visual, auditory, and kinesthetic.

◆ specific situations prior to or during a match.

◆ your emotions or feelings associated with those specific situations.

◆ your thoughts and perceptions about the situations.

◆ the muscular sensations you use in those situations.

Understanding the factors that either inhibit and enhance your self-confidence allows you to be in a good position to make changes to build effective actions into your daily routines.

Learn what factors inhibit or enhance your self-confidence.

Steps to monitor your senses

Here are some steps to take to monitor your senses, prior to and during competitive play:

Step 1

Identify the specific situations where you seem to be at your lowest self-confidence level. These may be ones before match situations: when you are ready to go to the court, while you are waiting, during warmup with an opponent before the match, or when you begin play.

Or they could be specific situations in a game: winning the first point of a game, winning the last point of a game, at crucial breakpoints, or during changeovers. In short, any situation that causes you to lose confidence.

Learn to identify the situations in which you have the least amount of self-confidence.

Step 2

Once the specific situations have been identified that seem to relate to low self-confidence, you now can more easily determine the emotions or feelings that occur in those situations. Usually, these will be emotions that can be described as fear, worry, or doubt.

These are emotions that many times have to do with the fact that you do not know what the outcome of a particular situation will be. As a result, you are more likely to question your ability to execute technically or mentally. Therefore, your self-confidence can be compromised.

You lose perspective on the active "here and now" situation. Fear, worry, and doubt can escalate as your self-confidence is lowered or otherwise inhibited. In determining your feelings, try to be as precise as possible as to what they are, what they feel like, and when they occur.

Once you have identified your low confidence situations, learn to associate the feelings that are associated with them.

Step 3

In addition to determining your negative emotional states, determine the thoughts and perceptions you have about the particular situation.

Usually these will be negative self-statements (e.g., I can't do anything right; no matter what I do, it won't work; I can't win) or negative perceptions (e.g., your opponent is perceived by you as intimidating; all of the close calls are going against you).

Learn what negative statements you may be associating with a particular situation.

Step 4

You also can identify any particular muscular sensations you experience during low confidence situations. Generally, these muscular sensations are likely to be reflected as tense or rigid muscles. The sensations may relate to certain muscle groups (e.g., shoulder or back), or the sensations may be experienced throughout your entire body. In any respect, try to identify particular sensations as they relate to certain situations.

Muscle sensations can also be identified and associated with particular low confidence states.

Monitor for enablers of self-confidence

In addition to monitoring your senses for negative situations, feelings, thoughts, perceptions, and muscular sensations, you can also determine the positive factors associated with each situation or event in your life—either on or off the court. In doing so, you are monitoring your senses to detect enablers of self-confidence.

Learn to monitor your senses during and before competitive play.

You can do this in the same manner as described above with respect to competitive play.

◆ Identify the specific situations in which you consider yourself to be highest in self-confidence.

◆ Determine the positive feelings that you have that make you self-confident in these specific situations.

◆ Determine the thoughts and perceptions that occur when you have these positive emotions.

◆ Describe your muscular sensations. These should be feelings of your muscles being loose, strong, and powerful.

Eliminate the negative and enhance the positive

When you monitor your senses before and during competitive play, you will detect aspects of your senses that limit your self-confidence and also aspects that build it up. With this information, you can take actions to eliminate the negative and enhance the positive.

To do so, it is important to understand how you use your breathing, how you relax, and how you cope with negative and unwanted thoughts that can influence your self-confidence.

Methods and procedures to do these things are discussed next.

Learn to use breathing to your advantage in practice and match play.

6. Use breathing to your advantage.

The manner in which you breathe during practice and competitive play has an effect on your self-confidence. The pattern of how you breathe will be different when you are relaxed, calm, and positive than when you as tense, anxious, and in other negative or stressful states.

You will be able to increase your self-confidence by learning to use breathing to your advantage. With practice, you can learn to regulate your breathing so that you can reach and maintain a relaxed, calm, positive state. Consequently, your self-confidence will be enhanced and maintained along with your overall mental efficiency.

Practice Breathing Techniques

You can learn to regulate your own breathing, which will increase your self-confidence.

Here is a procedure you can follow to learn and practice breathing techniques in order to regulate breathing to your advantage when playing tennis.

1. You can practice inhaling—taking a deep breath slowly and systematically through your nostrils. When you do this, relax, and do not strain yourself. Inhale to a count of 4.

2. Before exhaling this breath, take a brief pause of about 5 seconds. As you do so, feel your entire body relax and feel energetic, in a positive state. Imagine yourself performing on the tennis court the way that you want to—in a specific manner—such as hitting a winning passing shot.

3. Then, exhale slowly and continuously through your mouth. Do this up to a count of 7 to 9 or 10. Again, feel yourself being in a relaxed or positive state. Think about yourself playing tennis in a quality way.

Slow down your rate of breathing

Use breathing to relax and eliminate negative and unproductive performance states.

The above procedure is designed to slow down your rate of breathing. When you are preparing to play tennis or actually are doing so and you feel anxious, tense, or intimidated, you can apply the above procedure. You also can use it when you begin to recognize that you are starting to get into a negative state.

7. Learn to relax.

When you are in a relaxed state, you are able to control the tension of your muscles. This allows you to be in better physical control, more composed, and in control of yourself mentally. In doing this, you can learn to reach a more self-confident condition.

To realize these states, however, you need to learn how to regulate two things about yourself.

1 First, you need to be able to control what you think.

2 Second, you need to be able to detect the differences in the tension in your muscles. This involves knowing when there are increases and decreases in muscle tension in all muscles throughout your body. To acquire this ability, you need to learn how to control and relax your muscles by practicing progressive relaxation.

You need to be able to control what you think and able to detect the differences in your muscle tension.

Progressive Relaxation Procedure

Here is one progressive relaxation procedure that you can practice. It will take you about 10 minutes.

1. Locate a room that is quiet and where you will not be disturbed by anyone while you are practicing the progressive relaxation procedure. Make sure that you have a comfortable chair or you can be on the floor instead of sitting in a chair.

2. To begin, close both of your eyes and begin to engage in the breathing procedure that we discussed above for about a minute or so. As you take these breaths with your eyes closed, feel yourself relaxing—"letting yourself go"—into a positive and composed state.

3. Next, extend both your arms. Now, clench your fists. As you do this, gradually increase the tension levels in your fists. Increase this tension until your hands are fully tight.

   Now, gradually relax the tension in your hands. Let your arms drop naturally to your sides as you release

Practicing progressive relaxation will help you learn how to control and relax your muscles.

Become aware of the differences in your muscles when you are feeling tense and when you are feeling relaxed.

the tension. As you do this, become aware of the differences in your muscles when you are feeling tense and when you are feeling relaxed. Be aware of these differences for all other progressive relaxation exercises below.

4. Now, use these steps for each of the following muscles or muscle groups:
   - tense the muscles
   - hold the tension on the muscles
   - become aware of the tension in the muscles
   - relax the tension
   - become aware of the relaxed state

   Apply this procedure for the following muscle groups:
   - muscles of your lower arm and elbow
   - muscles in your forehand and face
   - muscles in your neck
   - shoulders, upper back, lower back
   - chest
   - abdomen
   - upper legs
   - lower legs
   - feet and toes

Practice the progressive relaxation procedure on a regular basis.

5. Now concentrate on relaxing the muscles of your body. In particular, become aware of any areas of your body that still are tense in any way. Then, relax those areas again.

6. Open your eyes. You should stretch and feel refreshed.

Relaxing your muscles quickly takes practice

You should practice the progressive relaxation procedure on a regular basis. In relation to learning how to relax your muscles, determine for yourself how relaxed you need to be to achieve maximum quickness, power, and accuracy in your game.

As you become more skilled at relaxation of your muscles, you should try to get your muscles to relax quickly without having to bring your muscle groups to a full state of relaxation.

You can accomplish this by practicing until you get to the point where you can relax your muscles quickly just by thinking certain thoughts and seeing certain images.

8. Use thought control.

Learn to control your thoughts to improve your self-confidence.

You also can help yourself remain self-confident by learning to control your thoughts. In doing so, make sure you keep your thoughts positive and minimize or eliminate negative thoughts.

A positive thought is one that provides you with a clear and useful way of doing something well. For instance, when you think about playing in a big match, and having fun while you play, you are thinking in a positive and productive manner. This type of positive thought will help boost or maintain your self-confidence.

Negative thoughts can adversely affect your game both mentally and physically.

In contrast, a negative thought is one that provides you with an image or picture of not doing well. Negative thoughts are associated with feelings of anxiety. When you see yourself, for example, not being able to return your opponent's serve effectively, and you become apprehensive or anxious about it, you have a negative thought present that is likely to limit your self-confidence. This will especially be true during competitive play.

When you focus on negative thoughts, ones that are disturbing and anxiety-producing, you will be out of balance both mentally and physically. In essence, you will be mentally *inefficient*.

You will have a difficult time focusing or concentrating on any aspect of the match. This occurs because you become distracted and in a diminished self-confident state.

Learn to say "no" to negative thoughts.

However, when you focus on positive thoughts and work to eliminate any negative thoughts that come to your mind, you will be able to concentrate more effectively and be more confident about yourself and how you play. In this regard, you will be mentally efficient.

Steps to controlling your thoughts

There are several steps you can take to control your thoughts while you practice and play competitively. You can use these steps at any time—both on and off the court—during practice and match play. These steps are:

Step 1

Focus your mind on a positive thought.

When a negative thought enters your mind, use the thought-stopping procedure of just saying "no" to the thought. This is the same approach you would use if you said "no" to someone who wanted you to do something that was of no interest to you or that you felt would be harmful to you.

Step 2

Once you have said no to the negative thought, rapidly focus your mind on a positive thought. This will help center your attention on the positive and make you feel better as well.

Step 3

Use the technique of "letting go" of the negative thought.

When you are off the court, you also can use the technique of "letting go" of the negative thought. You simply disregard the thought, let the thought go, and do not focus on it. Feel it leave your mind. Then think about something that is more pleasant and productive. Congratulate yourself on the wise decision you made to focus on a positive, rather than a negative, thought.

Remind yourself that you can control your thoughts and make them positive.

Step 4

Tell yourself on a regular basis that you can control your thoughts. In fact, take pride in your ability to do so. Remember, do not let thoughts influence you and your self-confidence, except for the positive ones that you choose.

Tell yourself on a regular basis that you can control your thoughts and make them positive.

CHAPTER SUMMARY

In this chapter, we focused on building and maintaining your self-confidence as a personal quality of the mentally efficient tennis player. We discussed the need for you to remain in a self-confident state—both on and off the tennis court—and to be aware of your levels of confidence.

We noted several personal benefits you can gain by being self-confident and certain problems that can be prevented through your self-confidence.

Then we discussed Step 3 of the Mental Efficiency Program: Build and maintain confidence in yourself.

Let go of all negative thoughts from your mind.

Last, we detailed procedures for you to use in undertaking this step successfully:

◆ Establish an agreement with yourself.

◆ Assess your self-confidence.

◆ Know your current level of skill.

◆ Appraise your situations and results realistically.

◆ Monitor your senses.

◆ Use breathing to your advantage.

◆ Learn to relax.

◆ Use thought control.

We will now discuss the personal quality of self-discipline, another one of the basic building blocks of mental efficiency.

5

POSSESSING

SELF-DISCIPLINE

Boris Becker, Nick's protégé

The will to win is important, but the will to prepare is vital.

Joe Paterno
Penn State Football Coach

Push yourself again and again. Don't give an inch until the final buzzer sounds.

Larry Bird
Boston Celtics Basketball Player

Paralyze resistance with persistence.

Woody Hayes
Ohio State Football Coach

Boris Becker—as of this writing—has had a 9-year career beginning as the youngest player to ever win at Wimbledon. He was only 17. Now he has won six Grand Slams and become a hero in Germany. Players and nonplayers alike worldwide know him as the player who will not let a ball go by whether he has to dig a tunnel, jump to the moon, or eat a mouthful of court. As an early champion, he had an uphill battle to continue to perform as well, or better, (can you do better than winning Wimbledon at 17?) to remain at the lofty height set by the "tennis world" and his following.

Many times, athletes who have had early success in their careers sometimes come to a point where they lose some of their excitement and momentum.

As they mature and find more of the world, they reflect on all that is out there and the opportunity that may exist for them.

I think, to a certain extent, this is true of Boris (as it may have been with Bjorn Borg). He had new opportunities and interests. He was growing and maturing. Certainly his new family is an entirely unique concept for him that demands his attention and time. He must balance his priorities and decide what he wants.

When a world class athlete—who is among a very few that have the ability to be the best—loses their focus (fire or drive) for their work, dry spells can occur and sometimes can never be broken.

When I began with Boris in late 1993, my first question to Boris was "Do you want to play tennis and reach the level you once held?" His answer was "Yes, Yes, Yes!" He renewed his initial fire and worked harder than he ever had in his life with one purpose in mind: to regain his rightful place in tennis history.

Boris had to reevaluate his goals and reset his priorities. He had to decide whether he again wanted to pay the price to be his best. The standards and rules Becker had to set offered no limitations. He had to form a game plan much different than his first run to the top. His obligations had increased along with his age and the competition. He was no longer a young boy with few responsibilities and obligations, but rather a married man and father, a multimillionaire businessman with the German nation watching, waiting for, and wanting his return.

In true German fashion, his efforts were calculated. He made a decision to gain back his position in the tennis world. He chose his team, leaving no area of development untouched. He established a work schedule involving practice and match play, pushing his abilities and strength to the limit. He scheduled his events in a periodic manner to peak at the most important and appropriate times. He balanced his personal and tennis life. He made a decision, formed a game plan, and worked for the execution. He didn't look back.

Nick Bollettieri

5 | POSSESSING SELF-DISCIPLINE

WHAT'S IN THIS CHAPTER

In this chapter, we will discuss how you can develop and possess self-discipline to help you be the best tennis player—and person—possible.

Self-discipline is your ability to effectively master three separate, yet interrelated activities. These are:

1. Initiating personal actions toward goals you want to accomplish. This generally involves personal plans.

2. Following through on your plans despite setbacks.

3. Making adjustments on how you follow through to be more effective in reaching your established goals.

Serious athletes are disciplined in their sport and in other areas of their lives.

Based on our research with tennis players and other performers, most athletes who have reached a certain level of high proficiency in sport and competition are disciplined in their sport as well as in other areas of their lives.

WHY YOU NEED SELF-DISCIPLINE

If you know what you want to accomplish in tennis both short and long term, you have already taken a positive first step in attaining your goals. Being aware of yourself and setting personal goals will help you become and remain motivated. In addition, knowing what you want to accomplish will also help you be a self-disciplined individual and mentally efficient tennis player.

MAKING NECESSARY ADJUSTMENTS

Knowing what you want to accomplish and why you want to do so is a necessary—but not complete—condition for you to improve your tennis performance. In addition, you must be able to take personal actions and follow through on them. In other words, you need to be self-disciplined.

During tennis training for instance, your practice plan might involve personal actions such as drilling down the line on both sides for 10 minutes each into the back half of the back court.

Or, you may practice serving and volleying in intervals of 10 points each with a practice partner. Or, you may focus on rearranging the strings in your racquet in between points to help in your relaxation and to maintain concentration.

These are personal actions that should be planned by you in advance to improve your performance or to allow you to concentrate directly on your performance.

ABILITY TO FOLLOW THROUGH

Self-discipline also involves being able to follow through on other things—both on and off the tennis court—on a routine basis. This could involve actions that reflect how you schedule and manage your time before practice and games, how you go about studying, and what you do to maintain a nutritious, balanced diet.

GAIN PERSONAL BENEFITS

There are several benefits that you gain from being self-disciplined. These benefits will help you to stay focused as you practice and during competitive match play. Moreover, there

When you plan out the actions you need to take to attain your goals and then follow through, making necessary adjustments along the way, you are actively involved in developing and possessing self-discipline.

Self-discipline involves following through on activities not directly related to your primary goal, yet important to accomplishing it.

will be "carryover" effects to other areas of your life that involve disciplining yourself such as in academic study, learning a musical instrument, or planning your summer.

Personal planning has several meaningful personal benefits.

1 The first benefit involves a clear recognition and sincere appreciation of the value of personal planning. When you plan out how you are going to proceed during an activity and then follow through with the actions, you are able to both understand and appreciate the actions and know what you have to do in order to accomplish them.

You have available specific information (a plan) to guide you toward your goals. Since this plan will help you to know what to do and how to do it, you will feel more disciplined, in personal control, and also more self-motivated and self-confident.

Being self-disciplined promotes positive and constructive thoughts and behaviors.

2 A second benefit from being self-disciplined is that each and every one of your personal plans, when thoughtfully constructed, allows you to focus and concentrate on positive thoughts, feelings, and behaviors that help you prevent negative ones from entering your situation.

As a result, the likelihood of your being able to sustain the follow through that is needed to attain your goals is increased.

For example, with a sound game plan, you can prepare for a match in a focused manner. Needless mental and physical energy will not be wasted by you prior to the match or during it. As a result, you contribute to your mental efficiency.

Being self-disciplined provides you with positive reinforcement.

3 Self-discipline also provides you with a third personal benefit. Through self-discipline, you develop habits and skills that are positive reinforcement. For example, most tennis players and other people gain much satisfaction from following through and accomplishing challenging activities.

When you derive personal satisfaction from something that you do—in this case, disciplining yourself to train and compete—you are more likely to persevere with those activities and goals even during difficult times and when you are faced with unforeseen obstacles. Consequently, you remain more poised and in positive control of your thoughts, emotions, and behaviors.

PREVENT PROBLEMS

Through effective self-discipline, you also will be able to prevent personal problems from occurring and to otherwise minimize any that may develop.

1 First, by planning out the effective actions you need to take, you are able to prevent time from being wasted. You will be able to avoid situations where you do things that do not contribute to your development or may, in some instances, be detrimental to your intentions.

Other benefits of self-discipline are using your time effectively, gaining a positive sense of self-control, and taking actions and moving forward – initiating positive and active change in your life.

2 Second, when you are able to discipline yourself effectively, you are able to develop a positive and realistic sense of personal control. When you are undisciplined, you may feel out of control—not able to manage your time or do the little things necessary for success. Consequently, you are likely to feel anxious, frustrated, and even angry.

3 Finally, through self-discipline, you are taking actions and moving forward; you are initiating positive change in your life.

Step 4

Initiate personal plans and follow through on them.

By taking this step, your chances of being a self-disciplined individual in relation to tennis and other areas of your life will be greatly increased. Some self-discipline development activities that you can participate in throughout the year include:

1. Commit yourself to personal plans and planning.

2. Plan your actions.

3. Discuss your plans with other people.

4. Monitor your follow-through.

5. Make necessary changes.

6. Reinforce yourself.

7. Use productive routines.

8. Use visualization.

9. Use positive affirmations.

Make a commitment to developing a personal plan.

Each one of these activities is discussed in the remainder of this chapter.

1. Commit yourself to personal plans and planning.

To have self-discipline, you must commit yourself to personal plans and to the process of personal planning. This means mapping out, as often as possible in written form, how you plan to accomplish your goals. A personal plan is a statement of the actions you will take to accomplish something.

Our experiences and research with successful tennis players, athletes in other sports, and people from all other walks of life show clearly the importance of personal plans and the process of personal planning.

A personal plan is a statement of the actions that you will take to accomplish something.

Four major plans

There are many types of personal plans. All of them are important to your mental efficiency as a tennis player and to your self-discipline. Four major types of personal plans are described here.

1. Long-range plan

This is a plan that is targeted to one or more of your long-range personal goals such as the types of tennis goals dis-

The implementation of a long-range plan for your tennis development will require you to be patient and to persevere as you make progress toward your goals.

cussed in Chapter 3 on self-motivation. The plan is called long-range because the actions you will need to take to attain your personal goals need to occur over the long term: a month, several months, or a year.

The length of time depends on the goal. If, for instance, you have a personal goal to develop an effective slice serve, the personal actions you will need to take to attain that goal must be implemented over a course of time—generally several months both during training and competition. Since there is no "quick-fix" in attaining this personal goal, the plan you need is a long-range one.

2. Game plan

This is a plan you develop to help you perform effectively during a particular match, against a certain opponent. This kind of plan includes one or more match goals—a strategy; and specific actions you need to take during the match to remain disciplined and to execute effectively—tactics.

A game plan includes one or more specific goals to be developed and implemented during match play. Game plans involve the use of strategy and tactics.

For example, if you have a serve and volley style of play, and your opponent is an aggressive baseline player, your game plan might focus on match goals and actions that would involve getting a high percentage of first serves in, using a short slice to bring your opponent to the net, and/or attacking your opponent's second serve consistently.

3. Off-season plan

This is a plan that focuses on how you can develop yourself during periods of the year in which you are not competitively active. This "periodization" procedure allows you to make changes in your game, rest mentally, and build toward competitive "peak" periods in the year.

An off-season plan is likely to include personal actions to help you acquire and develop your physical strength and condition or perhaps particular mental skills.

Off-season plans allow you to develop both physically and mentally in between competition to reach "peak" performance in a timed and planned manner. This is also called "periodization."

4. Continuing education plan

A continuing education plan is targeted to your development beyond and outside the area of tennis.

This kind of plan is targeted to development of yourself beyond and outside the area of tennis. A plan for your continuing education may include personal actions that will help you reach a certain level of education, such as a college degree, or enable you to go back to school following graduation from school for postgraduate studies or technical training.

You may need to develop other types of plans as they are relevant to you and your needs. The process of initiating these types of plans and following through on them is covered now in the remainder of this chapter.

2. Plan your actions.

You can effectively plan the actions that you need to take to attain any of your goals by using the process of personal planning.

All the goals and actions for your tennis and life can be planned.

This same process will apply to any type of goal or plan including long-range tennis goals and plans, match goals, and game plans, as well as goals and plans for your continuing education or development outside the area of tennis.

The process of personal planning is implemented by means of a series of separate, yet interrelated steps, as listed on page 113. These steps can be used in conjunction with Figure 5-1, entitled The Personal Planning Form (PPF), a copy of which is seen on the next page of this chapter.

Figure 5-1. Personal Planning Form (PPF)

Name_____Date_____Type of Plan_____

People to discuss this plan with:_____

Goals	Personal Actions	Timelines	Comments
I.			

Steps to personal planning

Step 1

Decide which kind of goals will be your target for a personal plan.

Decide which kind of goals will be your target for a personal plan. These kinds of goals may be (a) long-range tennis goals, reflecting physical and mental skills; (b) match goals; (c) goals for off-season development; and/or (d) continuing education goals.

Remember that there is a different plan required for each kind of goal. In this way, you will be able to more effectively discipline yourself because you will be able to specify particular actions that will result in goal attainment. Therefore, actions that are NOT likely to be effective or efficient can be eliminated from the plan.

Step 2

On the Personal Planning Form (PPF), list the goals on which your plan will focus.

List the goals on which your plan will focus in the spaces provided on the Personal Planning Form (PPF).

Step 3

Specify the personal actions you will take.

Now, specify the personal actions you will take that will enable you to make progress toward and attain each of your goals. Make sure you think through these personal actions very thoroughly so that you are clear with yourself as to just what these actions are and how you believe they will be effective. List these actions on the PPF in the space provided.

Step 4

Record a particular date or period of time in which you need to undertake and complete the action.

For each personal action you have now listed on the PPF, record a particular date or period of time in which you need to undertake and complete the action. By recording this time-referenced information, you will be able to increase your focus and concentration. This will also enhance your self-discipline and contribute to your mental efficiency.

Make sure you have a way of knowing when the personal actions that you have listed are completed.

Step 5

Make sure you have a way of knowing when the personal actions that you have listed are completed. If you need some form of evidence to make the determination—such as a checksheet or record of practice sessions completed—describe that information under the comments sections of the PPF.

Step 6

Once you have placed the above information on the PPF, think about any obstacles that may present themselves as you follow through on the plan. These obstacles are generally personal in nature and are under your control.

They might include (a) negative thinking on your part that you will not be able to follow through; (b) feelings of fear, worry, and doubt about not being successful in implementing the plan; (c) a tendency on your part to put off taking certain actions; and (d) any other obstacles that have to do with how you behave or relate to other people.

Describe any personal obstacles under the comments section of the PPF.

Step 7

Describe any personal obstacles under the comments section of the PPF, next to the goal or goals to which the obstacle relates. Next to each obstacle, comment on how you will overcome it. You may prefer to describe these obstacles and solutions on a separate sheet of paper. This sheet, then, can be attached to the PPF.

List the people with whom you expect to discuss the plan.

Step 8

List the people with whom you expect to discuss the plan.

Figures 5-2, 5-3, and 5-4 illustrate completed personal plans that have been developed using the process of personal planning described above.

Figure 5-2. Personal Planning Form (PPF)
Example of completed plan targeted to long-range tennis goals

Name_____*Jose Lambert*_____Date__*3/25*_____Type of Plan__*Long-range*_____

People to discuss this plan with:_____*Tennis Coach*_____

Goals	Personal Actions	Timelines	Comments
1. *Improve B-H top-spin down the line*	•*Use rally drills and passing shot drills* •*Count to 10 when I make an unforced error*	*Monday, Wednesday, Friday*	*Have my teammate help me to follow through with this drill*
2. *Improve B-H volley down the line*	•*Use the volley to the corner drill and repetition drills* •*Use the thought-stopping method to eliminate my poor self-talk*	*Daily*	*Monitor the quality of my efforts at visualization*
3. *Improve slice serve to deuce court*	•*Use visualization and progressive relaxation*	*Daily*	*Obtain necessary equipment*
4. *Improve B-H slice approach shot*	•*Use the approach shot drill* •*Review my performance videotape*	*Friday*	
5. *Improve B-H top-spin down the line passing shot*	•*Take 50 practice shots with partner fielding the ball*	*Daily*	*Thank my practice partner for his/her assistance*

Figure 5-3. Personal Planning Form (PPF)
Example of completed plan targeted to match goals

Name _Lisa Smith_ Date _7/14_ Type of Plan _Match (Game Plan)_

People to discuss this plan with: _Tennis Coach; Team Captain_

Goals	Personal Actions	Timelines	Comments
1. Getting in a high percentage of first serve shots (my opponent is an aggressive base-liner)	•Use visuals (strings, towel)	Prematch and during the competition	Make time for my prematch work; get there early
2. Use a short slice to bring my opponent to the net	•Stay balanced and focused	All the time	Monitor myself during changeovers
3. Attack my opponent's second serve consistently	•Go right after the shot; stay focused and in control	Routinely	Last match this worked effectively

Figure 5-4. Personal Planning Form (PPF)
Example of completed plan targeted to continuing education goals

Name_____*Chris Bailey*_____Date___*11/2*_____Type of Plan_*Continuing Education*_

People to discuss this plan with:_*Parents; Guidance Counselor; Tennis Coach*_____

Goals	Personal Actions	Timelines	Comments
1. *Learn about colleges and universities in the southwest (especially those that have contacted me for scholarships)*	• *Meet with school guidance counselor* • *Review computer files in guidance office* • *Meet with college representatives*	*October* *By November 19*	*Set the exact appointment date and time*
2. *Prepare effectively for the SAT*	• *Take the SAT preparation courses* • *Review my algebra and English notes*	*September and October*	
3. *Make appropriate selection of college*	• *Use the checklist that I received at the college seminar* • *Discuss with my parents* • *Visit my short list of colleges*	*December and January*	*Set visitation schedule dates*

3. Discuss your plans with other people.

You can develop and improve your self-discipline by discussing each of your personal plans with other people. These people should be ones whose judgments you trust and whom you respect. In turn, they should be supportive of your development as a tennis player. More specifically, you may want to discuss your personal plans with one or more of the following:

- Your tennis coach or professional consultant

- Your parents

- Another tennis player who is qualified to help you (e.g., an older player, team captain)

- A teacher or counselor in school

It is valuable to have others critique and support your plan.

Two things that will happen

When you discuss a personal plan with other people as outlined above, two things are likely to happen that relate to your self-discipline.

1 You will encourage other opinions about your plan. Perhaps you may have overlooked some goal, personal action, or obstacle that they can point out to you. This will allow you to make any required changes in the plan.

2 You will have announced your plan to other people by talking about it with them. You now have someone who is knowledgeable and supportive of your plan—a person who can prompt you periodically to make sure you are following through on your plans. In addition, they can provide you with recognition, praise, and other forms of positive feedback when you implement your personal actions.

How to discuss your personal plans

Below are some activities you can use to discuss any of your personal plans with others.

Activity 1

When you first meet with the individual, explain that you are not only attempting to achieve certain goals but that you are also going to use the process of personal planning to be a more self-disciplined individual.

This explanation will set the tone and focus for the session.

Activity 2

Show another person your plan and discuss it in detail with them.

Provide the individual with a copy of the Personal Planning Form (PPF) that you have completed by yourself. Although the type of plan will be stated on the PPF, it is important to make sure that the individual is aware of exactly why you have chosen the goals and listed the actions on the PPF.

Activity 3

Go over each of the personal actions you have listed in relation to the various goals. Explain to the individual your reasons for planning these actions. Make sure to comment on the timelines as well.

Activity 4

Seek this individual's constructive criticism as well as their comments about your plan.

Now, discuss any obstacles you have identified and why you think they might occur as you follow through on the plan. Discuss proposed solutions or ways to get around the obstacles. Consider how you will monitor yourself in following through on your plan.

Activity 5

Seek the advice and opinion of the individual about your plan. Ask them if they find the plan to be clear and appropriate. Determine whether they find anything missing that should be included in the plan, like additional goals, personal actions, or recognition of obstacles. Ask them their rationale for these changes.

Activity 6

Thank the person for their time, interest, and support. Ask them if they wish to receive a copy of a revised plan and to further discuss it with you.

Activity 7

Revise the plan as required.

Activity 8

Keep in contact with the person based on their willingness to provide you with periodic advice and support.

4. Monitor your follow-through.

**Take a
systematic
approach to
monitoring
yourself.**

You can enhance your self-discipline by monitoring your follow-through on a personal plan. The process of monitoring, in and of itself, is known to be an effective way of disciplining yourself.

This is true because when you "watch yourself" do something, like following through on a personal action to train at least four times a week, you will increase your chances of completing your plan.

We recommend that you take a systematic approach to monitoring yourself in relation to a personal plan. This involves using a rating scale, troubleshooting reasons for any performance problems you detect, and then making decisions about necessary changes in your game.

Take a systematic approach

For any plan, you can monitor yourself in a systematic way as follows:

Step 1

On a routine basis, give yourself a rating on the extent to which you believe you have followed through on each one of your personal actions that you have listed as part of your plan on the PPF. You can rate yourself by using a scale where 1 = Excellent, 2 = Good, 3 = Average, 4 = Fair, 5 = Poor.

Step 2

For personal actions where you have given yourself a relatively high rating (e.g., "1" or "2"), you can make a personal commitment with yourself to continue following through in a high quality way.

If you are not satisfied with how you have followed through, you can "troubleshoot" possible reasons.

Step 3

For any personal action that you rated yourself as average (e.g., "3") or less than average (e.g., "4" and "5"), you need to determine the reasons for those ratings to improve the quality of your actions. In this regard, if you are not satisfied with how you have followed through, you can "troubleshoot" possible reasons. These reasons may be one or more of the following:

◆ You did not actually implement the action because you forgot about it.

◆ You did not follow through on the action because you put it off (procrastinated).

◆ You did not follow through because once you got started, you simply did not know how to proceed.

◆ You developed general feelings of disinterest in the action.

◆ Other reasons.

Use the information from your troubleshooting activity to make changes in your plan.

Step 4

You can use the information from your troubleshooting activity to make changes in your plan or to make a personal commitment to do a better job in following through with your plan.

You not only can get this information from your own observation of yourself but also from the feedback supplied by your coach or other people who are knowledgeable with and have agreed to help you with your plan.

Step 5

You also can make similar ratings as above on the extent to which you have persevered in following through on your plan and overcome obstacles along the way. You can also troubleshoot reasons for any low ratings and make changes as necessary.

5. Make necessary changes.

Don't be afraid to make changes if they are warranted and necessary to affect the outcome of a performance or action.

Self-discipline does not mean that you never make a change in your personal plans. Rather, when you are an effective self-disciplined individual, you are constantly monitoring the extent to which you are following through, identifying obstacles and problems as you play, and making the changes that are necessary to accomplish your goals.

For example, you might have a game plan against a particular opponent in which you intend to use an aggressive baseline approach. As the match proceeds, however, you notice that your opponent is coming into the net as often as possible.

Flexibility is an indicator of a self-disciplined approach as well as a mentally efficient tennis player.

Rather than play a steady strategy waiting for your opponent to miss, you mix up passing shots with lobs and are able to force your opponent into making errors by playing a game that they are not adept at.

In changing your game plan, you have been able to adapt to a new situation and are successful in doing so. This kind of flexibility is an indicator of a self-disciplined approach as well as a mentally efficient tennis player.

Reasons for changes

There are several reasons why you may need to make necessary changes in your personal plans whether they are long-range plans, game plans for competitive play, or other types of plans. These reasons are listed below.

Actions are not working

Find the most effective and efficient means to achieve your actions and goals.

The actions that you have been using up to a certain point in a match are not getting the results you want. For instance, you may not be attaining your match goals, and a change in your court tactics is warranted during the match; otherwise, you are not likely to win.

A more efficient way

The actions you have been taking are effective. However, you have found an even more efficient way to get the same results. For example, you may have begun to use a new strength and conditioning method that has increased the muscle mass in your legs with less workout time.

Side effects

Although you are following through on your plan, you have detected some side effects that you did not anticipate.

You may have to readjust the time period for attaining a goal.

For example, in working toward a tennis goal, you determine that the amount of time you are spending on it has affected your school achievement to the point of failing some of your subjects. You now must readjust the time period in which you are likely to attain the goal. Perhaps, you will need to move the timeline to include another six months.

Other reasons

You may use other reasons that have to do with yourself, school, or family. By coordination of how you monitor yourself (discussed above) and being ready and able to make necessary changes, you will be that much more of a self-disciplined player and individual.

6. Reinforce yourself.

The task of initiating a personal plan and following through on it can take some time. In addition, when you persevere and make necessary changes in a plan, you really are expending valuable time and energy.

When you do these things, you want to be able to keep a positive momentum; you do not want your efforts at following through to become exhausting. You want, of course, to maximize your mental efficiency.

One way to increase the likelihood that you will follow through on your plans, persevere in spite of obstacles and setbacks, and make necessary changes is by means of self-reinforcement.

Self-reinforcement means that you do something to yourself that you consider to be a positive experience.

Self-reinforcement means that you do something to yourself that you consider to be a positive experience.

As a result of the positive experience, you are satisfied, feel good or, in more technical terms, are reinforced. The likelihood is increased that you will continue to make sure that you follow through and attain your goals.

Ways to reinforce yourself

There are a variety of actions that you can take to reinforce yourself and that can assist you in becoming a highly self-disciplined tennis player and person. Here are some things for you to consider:

Action 1

When you follow through and do something—complete a difficult practice session—take a few minutes to reflect on the experience.

Compliment and reward yourself for a job well done. Also enjoy reinforcement from others.

Feel a sense of satisfaction from knowing you did something that you might not otherwise have finished. Compliment yourself for a job well done.

Action 2

Take personal satisfaction in crossing off something that you have completed on your written personal plan or notebook. Just the behavior of crossing the item off the list is likely to be a reinforcing process for yourself.

Action 3

A routine is a standard way of doing something that helps contribute to your overall effectiveness.

Develop a sense of satisfaction just by knowing that you are making progress toward your goal. To develop this sense of satisfaction, you need to have a routine for monitoring your progress. Without this routine, it will be difficult to have your progress be a self-reinforcer because you will not know where you started and how far you have come.

Action 4

Once in a while, especially for major events or actions such as completing a match against a difficult opponent, reward yourself with something tangible or material.

Once in a while, reward yourself with something tangible or material.

This reward could be something as simple as taking a day off to spend with your friends; having dinner out; buying some new clothes or a new piece of equipment; taking a private lesson; or doing anything else that you consider to be reinforcing and that will help you follow through better the next time out.

Action 5

If you enjoy praise and recognition for a job well done, such as from your coach or parents, take a few moments out to think about and enjoy these positive comments. Do not become too enamored by the comments; feel good about the praise, and then get ready to move on.

Action 6

Be aware of other things that create a sense of satisfaction that can be used for self-reinforcement.

7. Use productive routines.

With respect to playing tennis, routines have to do with the typical or routine way you go about thinking (e.g., trying to focus on the positive in things), how you are likely to experience or feel when things happen (e.g., trying to stay composed during match play), and how you usually behave and move about on the court (e.g., what you do when you are getting ready for your opponent to serve).

Routines help you maintain self-discipline, sense of balance, and order in your day.

On a daily basis, having routines for doing things like serving, practicing, studying, or lifting weights helps you maintain self-discipline. Routines help you maintain a sense of balance and order in your day.

Build routine activities into your schedule

A productive routine is one that helps you take and follow through on your personal actions to attain your goals. A productive routine helps you know what you have to do on a regular basis, such as what activities are scheduled for you each day of the week.

A productive routine is one that helps you take and follow through on your personal actions to attain your goals.

By being able to predict what you need to do routinely to assure your success, you are in a good position to build these things into your daily schedules. These things might include time for study, watching videotapes, engaging in quality practices, or other actions and procedures that you need to do on a routine basis.

Routines are usually developed around certain life areas. From our experiences and research with tennis players and other performers, effective routines can be developed and used for the following:

Routines are usually developed around certain life areas.

- ◆ Maximizing the time you have at your disposal.
- ◆ Coping effectively with interpersonal situations that you will encounter on a daily basis.
- ◆ Specifying the information you need to have available to make decisions.

◆ Keeping in contact with family life and friends.

◆ Other areas and events.

Steps to making sure your routines are productive

You can do several things to make sure you have productive routines for the important areas of your life, especially as they affect your performance and progress as a tennis player. Toward this end, here is what you can do:

Step 1

Identify the personal areas of your life that are meaningful to your daily effectiveness in tennis and school. They are specific areas that are important to you and that, if left neglected or unattended in terms of productive routines, will minimize your effectiveness as a tennis player.

Identification, development, and use of routines in relation to these areas can help make sure you "remain balanced," each and every day—mentally, emotionally, and physically.

Here are some areas that may be personal to you and that may require you to develop and use productive daily routines:

◆ Time – the amount of time that is available during the day for you to realize your personal goals; the amount of other formal time that can be used for practice purposes; the time that is "nonnegotiable" for practice and other tennis functions.

◆ Your perception of situations – any situation can be perceived in a positive or negative way, or in a more neutral manner. In this regard, you have the option of how any situation is perceived. For instance, is the situation of learning to go from a two-hand to a one-hand shot perceived by you as a challenge—and as a commitment—or as a source of stress?

◆ Information – the data that are quantified and qualified

Identify the personal areas of your life that are important to your daily effectiveness in tennis and school.

You have the option of perceiving a situation as a challenge or as a source of stress.

Figure 5-5. Routine Evaluation Form

Name_____Date_____

For each item below, give yourself a rating in the space provided to the left of each item. Use this rating scale: 1 = Excellent
2 = Good
3 = Average
4 = Fair
5 = Poor

____ 1. Overall, I am able to manage my time.

____ 2. I devote adequate time to study that allows me to be successful in school.

____ 3. I do not put off what I am supposed to do in school.

____ 4. I am able to make sure that I am ready to train in a quality manner.

____ 5. I can prepare for matches efficiently.

____ 6. I am able to add and include appointments in my schedule without any difficulty.

____ 7. I am able to say no to people and decline to do things when time does not permit.

____ 8. I do not take on more things than I can handle.

____ 9. I am able to plan out a weekly schedule for my life.

____ 10. I spend quality time with family and friends.

and that allow you to make decisions about your progress as a tennis player or as a student (e.g., number of first serves in, number of unforced errors).

◆ Socialization – the ways in which you relate to your team, peers, coach, teachers, opponents, and others (e.g., formal meetings, practice sessions).

◆ Family Life – the quality, quantity, and nature of involvement with family members and other relevant people.

◆ Other areas that are relevant to you.

Step 2

Assess your current routines in relation to the above areas that you have identified. You can use the Routine Evaluation Form, seen as Figure 5-5.

Step 3

This step involves making the necessary explicit changes in particular daily routines so that you can manage yourself and the area more efficiently as a tennis player. You can then implement the changes and monitor yourself relative to those revisions.

Step 4

Evaluate the productiveness of your routines on a scheduled basis. Every week or two, you are encouraged to "make a routine appointment" with yourself (put it in your schedule book).

At this time, you can review how you have gone about dealing/coping with your important personal areas in your life and decide how effective you think your routines have been for you.

Assess your current routines in relation to the areas that you have identified.

Make changes in your routines as necessary.

Evaluate the productiveness of your routines on a scheduled basis.

Step 5

Make changes in your routines, based on your evaluation of them. You take a positive step toward mental efficiency when you make a change in a routine based on sound information about the routine's effectiveness.

8. Use visualization.

You can use the process of visualization to help you become and remain a self-disciplined tennis player and person.

Here are some procedures you can follow to use visualization in support of your self-discipline:

Procedure 1

Identify images of yourself functioning as a self-disciplined tennis player. In this regard, these images of self-discipline should be ones where you see yourself following through, making adjustments during competition, or any other situation in which you visualize yourself in a self-disciplined way.

Procedure 2

Describe and write down these images on a piece of paper so that you will know exactly what you are picturing about yourself. In addition, you can record a verbal description of these images on audiotape. Then, you can listen to these descriptions as a stimulus for your visualization of them.

Procedure 3

Visualize these images of effective self-discipline on a regularly scheduled basis. Make sure you know what you are visualizing and why you are doing so.

Reasons to use images

Here are several reasons to develop these kinds of images:

◆ To help motivate you to become and remain disciplined for a particular event or action such as a practice session.

You can use the process of visualization to help you become and remain a self-disciplined tennis player and person.

Identify images of yourself functioning as a self-disciplined tennis player.

Describe and write down these images.

Visualize these images of effective self-discipline on a regularly scheduled basis.

◆ To help you become refocused during match play.

◆ To reinforce yourself after you have maintained a self-disciplined effort.

◆ Other reasons that are important to you.

Step 4

Decide when and where you will engage in visualization to help with your self-discipline.

The more precise you can be as to the times that you will use positive mental images of yourself, the more mentally efficient you will be.

9. Use positive affirmations.

In addition to visualization, you also can use positive affirmations to support your self-discipline. Follow similar procedures such as these:

Procedure 1

Identify three or four phrases that are stated in the positive and that affirm that you are a self-disciplined tennis player. Here are some examples:

- "I enjoy following through on my practice sessions, doing a quality job."

- "When I feel myself losing concentration during a match, I quickly and effectively regain focus."

- "I make rapid, powerful adjustments as I play my opponent."

Procedure 2

Write these positive self-statements down on a piece of paper. You can also use a tape recorder to listen to them in the future.

The more precise you can be as to the times that you will use positive images of yourself, the more mentally efficient you will be.

Use positive affirmations to support your self-discipline.

Procedure 3

Have a reason for wanting to use these self-statements for self-motivation, refocusing, and/or self-reinforcement.

Procedure 4

Decide when and where you will use these positive statements about your self-discipline.

CHAPTER SUMMARY

In this chapter, we focused on your self-discipline. In doing so, we discussed the personal benefits derived when you are self-disciplined and the problems that can be prevented by your possessing self-discipline.

We then focused on Step 4 of the Mental Efficiency Program: Initiate personal plans and follow through on them.

Finally, we detailed how to engage in the following activities in support of your self-discipline:

- ◆ Commit yourself to personal plans and planning.
- ◆ Plan your actions.
- ◆ Discuss your plans with other people.
- ◆ Monitor your follow-through.
- ◆ Make necessary changes.
- ◆ Reinforce yourself.
- ◆ Use productive routines.
- ◆ Use visualization.
- ◆ Use positive affirmations.

6

MAINTAINING

QUALITY

INTERPERSONAL

RELATIONSHIPS

Nick with friends—the Monte Hurowitz family of New York—and daughter Danielle.

The secret is to work less as individuals and more as a team. As a coach, I play not my eleven best, but my best eleven.

Knute Rockne
University of Notre Dame Football Coach

Many heads, hearts, and minds generally contribute to anyone's notable achievements.

Walt Disney
American Animator and Film Producer

The most important single ingredient in the formula of success is knowing how to get along with people.

Theodore Roosevelt
26th President, United States of America

Without my friends, I would not be where I am today. A trite statement? Not at all. A bold statement? Certainly.

There is no question that I have built my life and my work with the help of my friends. They have believed in me no matter how crazy (not at all an understatement for Nick Bollettieri) my ideas may have been. They knew that what I wanted I would get, and they wanted to be part of the action—they are definitely part of the Nick Bollettieri story.

My life has had many ups and downs and many twists and turns. I have made and lost many fortunes, been married more than I would like to remember, and been scoffed at by my peers and the industry when my ideas ran counter to the tennis "tradition."

Through it all, my friends were always at my side. They alone seemed to understand and even beyond, to support me always. Some of the crazy ideas were just that—crazy. I tried to learn from these. Other ideas fared better and they speak for themselves every day in the hundreds of thousands of players who have been helped to play this great sport a little better; in the young lives that we have improved both on and, more important, off the court; in the friends that I have known and had faith.

Several families I touched through tennis have been with me my whole career. Their children are grown now—running their own businesses, in Congress, practicing medicine and law, teaching. What I was able to instill in their sons and daughters was something that they felt to be more valuable than all their wealth and power combined. And they recognized me for it and gave back when I reached out for their help. The Marxes, the Nelsons, the Hurowitzes, the Landows, the Engels, the Jack Snyders, Bernie Schmidt, Murray Evans, Tom Seavey, and many others have been invaluable to my life—they have

allowed me to be who I am and to have accomplished what I have. I will be indebted to them eternally.

There are others equally as important— a loyal staff of old friends—who have been with me and at my side throughout my entire career. They have seen the worst and the best of the Bollettieri times. They have suffered the abuse and the long hours, sacrificed their families, vacations, and personal lives, and experienced firsthand all the problems. They too have rightfully shared in the miracles and felt the pride of what we have accomplished together. Without them, we (I) would be back at Victory Park under the umbrella.

The sacrifice my family and children have had to make is enormous. It is very difficult for me to even think about. In spite of it all, they have been understanding and supportive. Being away from them for months at a time. The hours. All the growing up that I missed. This was not easy for us.

When it all shakes out, the friendships, associations, and networks that I have are my most prized possession. My interpersonal relationships have made it all worthwhile. I am nothing without them.

Nick Bollettieri

6 | MAINTAINING QUALITY INTERPERSONAL RELATIONSHIPS

WHAT'S IN THIS CHAPTER

In this chapter, we will discuss how you can develop and maintain quality, interpersonal relationships with other individuals both on and off the court. These people would include your coaches, teachers, teammates, the media, and others. This kind of relationship is also referred to as a mutually beneficial exchange. When effective, it is a win-win relationship for all involved.

The task of developing quality interpersonal relationships is essential to you as a mentally efficient tennis player and as a person. When you possess this personal quality, your life and performance—in and out of the sport of tennis—will be greatly enhanced.

WHY YOU NEED QUALITY INTERPERSONAL RELATIONSHIPS

If you want to accomplish something worthwhile in tennis and reach your personal best, you need the help of others. You cannot do it alone.

To increase your ability to reach your best, you must rely

> A quality interpersonal relationship refers to your ability to gain positive benefit from another human being, while providing that person with something valuable in return.

A quality interpersonal relationship is built on respect for another human being, trust in that person, and a sincere interest in helping them.

on other people. These people, in particular, may be your coaches and parents.

You need to rely on these people for personal advice, technical information about how to play the game (e.g., strategy deployment, stroke production), general guidance in how to balance tennis with other areas of your life, and for social and emotional support.

If you do not take advantage of these interpersonal opportunities, you will limit yourself in terms of quality information, human interaction, and tennis performance. Instead, you will be lessening your mental efficiency, both on and off the tennis court.

RELATING TO OTHERS IN A POSITIVE WAY

When you relate to someone else in a positive way, such as listening to their points of view without interrupting them, or thanking them for helping you, the chances are increased that the other person will act the same way toward you. As a result, you are likely to benefit from this personal experience, perhaps when you least expect to.

From our experiences in tennis and with other sports, we have observed a consistent pattern. The pattern is that when a player does not relate to other people in a positive way, it is likely that they will not perform well on the tennis court nor usually in other areas of life (e.g., school, work).

A ONE-WAY STREET

If you want to accomplish something worthwhile in tennis and reach your personal best, you need the help of others.

Players who have poor interpersonal relationships many times seem to want a "one-way street" all to themselves. They want something from another person, without being willing to give back anything in return. They seem to require things immediately and with "no strings attached."

On the tennis court, these players are likely to engage in behaviors such as consistently berating coaches and officials, cheating on line calls, or getting down on themselves when things are not going well during a game or when they lose a match. Consequently, they give up their opportunity to achieve quality tennis play. In essence, they lose more than a match—they may also lose their friends or other personal supporters.

MANY DIVERSE RELATIONSHIPS

Tennis is a sport that involves many diverse interpersonal relationships. Whether you are a top professional player, a collegian, junior, or club player, you probably have come in contact with many people. These people range from tennis officials, fans, friends, media, spectators, opponents, and many others.

Developing quality interpersonal relationships with all kinds of people, as well as knowing when not to associate with particular people, is a crucial, yet often neglected, personal need that can be effectively addressed when you are mentally efficient.

Developing quality interpersonal relationships with all kinds of people, as well as knowing when not to associate with particular people, is a crucial, yet often neglected, personal need that can be effectively addressed when you are mentally efficient.

GAIN PERSONAL BENEFITS

You can gain several benefits by developing and maintaining quality interpersonal relationships.

1 First, you can benefit by gaining the cooperation of other people, both individuals and groups, in the tennis area and beyond. When cooperation exists between two people, they will feel more positive and secure with one another.

It is important to gain the cooperation of others.

People are more likely to enjoy the process of interacting better than if there was little or no cooperation between them. When lack of cooperation exists, the people who are relating to one another become tense, anxious, distracted, and are more prone to be in a negative state, often without knowing it. Consequently, a valuable relationship does not result.

Helping others and being helped by others is a mutually profitable experience.

For example, when a tennis player is cooperating with his or her coach to find a better way of executing at the net—even if the solution is not immediately apparent to either of them—chances are that they will enjoy the process of solving the dilemma and eventually come to an effective solution. At the same time, they will have experienced a quality interpersonal relationship.

2 A second personal benefit for you when you develop and maintain quality interpersonal relationships is the satisfaction of being able to contribute to the development and progress of someone else.

This contribution may simply reflect the time you spend with another human being, the advice or suggestions that you give to that person, or seeing the results that were attained by an individual such as a teammate or doubles partner.

When you sense that you have contributed to another person, they will sense recognition of your help. Then both of you are likely to feel better about each other and you will feel better about yourself.

When respect for others and respect for yourself exist at the same time, you are more likely to enjoy playing tennis and practicing it.

3 The third benefit for maintaining quality interpersonal relationships has to do with respect. This dimension refers not only to the positive feelings obtained when you are able to respect other individuals—despite the situations and your opinion of them—but also the added benefit of respecting yourself.

When respect for others and respect for yourself exist at the same time, you are likely to enjoy playing tennis and practicing it more than if you had difficulties respecting others or yourself.

PREVENT PROBLEMS

Through establishing and maintaining quality interper-

You can eliminate and reduce a self-centered approach to your existence.

sonal relationships—both on and off the tennis court—you will be in a position to prevent several personal problems from occurring. When these problems are prevented, you are contributing to the positive development of your mental efficiency.

1 First, you can eliminate and reduce a self-centered approach to your existence. In this way, you are able to rise above the selfishness and jealousies that can occur when playing tennis.

You are better able to maintain quality relationships with various people.

2 Second, you are better able to maintain quality relationships with various people such as your parents, brothers and sisters, longstanding friends, and other people.

3 Third, you can prevent being disrespectful to the rights, needs, and well being of individuals and groups. People are similar, yet different. It is satisfying and proper to recognize and appreciate the diverse culture and ethnicity of the people with whom you are likely to come in contact.

You can prevent being disrespectful to the rights, needs, and well being of individuals and groups.

Step 5

Make your contacts with people quality experiences.

Make your contacts with people quality experiences.

By taking this step, you will maximize your chances of developing and maintaining quality interpersonal relationships and your mental efficiency. You will be more likely to experience quality interpersonal relationships—both on and off the tennis court. Quality interpersonal relationships will contribute to your mental efficiency in tennis and elsewhere. Various activities will help you maintain quality interpersonal relationships. These activities are:

1. Identify your personal network.

2. Take the lead in relating to others.

3. Accept personal feedback positively.

4. Provide personal feedback constructively.

5. Manage interpersonal conflict effectively.

The above activities are discussed in the remainder of this chapter.

1. Identify your personal network.

Your personal network consists of all the people who are important to you and with whom you want to maintain contact.

Your personal network consists of all the people who are important to you and with whom you want to maintain contact. When you identify your personal network of friends, family, and associates, you are in a position to take the lead to maintain quality interpersonal relationships with them.

Following are guidelines that you can use to identify your personal network.

What people?

Determine the actual people with whom you want to maintain quality interpersonal relationships.

Determine the actual people with whom you want to maintain quality interpersonal relationships. These individuals may include the following:

◆ Family members and loved ones – including parents, brothers, sisters, relatives, etc.

◆ Friends – these may include teammates but also individuals outside of the sport of tennis.

◆ Coaches and instructors – not only in tennis but in other areas such as personal training and in sports other than tennis.

◆ Teachers from schools or college.

◆ Other tennis associates – including opponents, former coaches, and teammates who are not your personal friends.

◆ Media and other members of the public – including reporters, tennis association officials.

◆ Other people who are important to you.

Categorize and record

Once you have identified the people you want to be part of your personal network, you can place them into various categories and record information about them in a personal directory, Rolodex file, or computer.

The information you record should serve as your basis for keeping in contact with each of these people in a quality way. In this regard, you may want to include some or all of the following information about each individual:

Place the people in your network in categories and record this information so it is readily available to you.

• Name and complete mailing address

• Telephone number and any relevant facsimile numbers

• Personal notes about birthdays, anniversaries, favorite music, places they like to eat, etc.

• Other information that is relevant to the individual that you want to record

Keep in touch

When you have recorded the information about each person, make sure you know how to keep in touch with each of them. Here are some questions to consider in this respect:

◆ When do I have an opportunity to contact this individual (e.g., holiday, weekly)?

◆ How do I want to keep in contact with this person (e.g., through exchange of holiday cards, monthly dinner meetings, telephone)?

◆ How will I make sure that I will maintain contact with them (e.g., place notes in my appointment book)?

Developing and maintaining quality interpersonal relationships can be enhanced when you take the initiative.

Maintain contacts

You now can make note of your answers to these questions and then proceed to follow through to maintain contacts with the people.

2. Take the lead in relating to others.

Developing and maintaining quality interpersonal relationships can be enhanced when you take the initiative. This means being able to know how you would like to benefit from others and how you can benefit them in return.

You can take the lead in relating to people by means of three separate—yet interrelated—activities described in detail below.

Specify your needs and interests

Specify your needs and interests in relation to other people with whom you want to have quality interpersonal relationships.

Specify your needs and interests in relation to other people with whom you want to have quality interpersonal relationships. The more specific you can be in terms of your needs and interests in relation to other people, the more likely you will know whether you are satisfied with each relationship you have with them. If you are clear with yourself as to what you would like to receive from another person in the way of a positive relationship, two things are likely to result.

1 First, you will understand what it is that you want.

2 Second, you will be in a better position to know if you have received it. Too often, we have found this lack of specific understanding to be at the root of interpersonal problems between a tennis player and his or her coach or some other relevant individual in their life. Therefore, the problem was maintained and the relationship deteriorated even further.

Ask and answer certain questions

You can specify your needs and interests in relation to other people in your personal network by asking and answering the following questions:

Determine your needs that can be fulfilled from your network of people.

◆ What would I like to receive from this individual that will help me develop as a tennis player and person?

◆ Why is receiving this help important to me?

In answering these questions, here are some examples of things that may be valuable to you from the various people in your network:

◆ Coach/Instructor – advice about game strategy, advice about mechanics, suggestions for eliminating mistakes, training programs, availability for practice, help with overall tennis play.

◆ Teachers – relevant knowledge, quick feedback on school projects and tasks, opportunities to ask questions to clarify homework assignments.

Specify the needs and interests of the other people with whom you want to maintain quality interpersonal relationships.

◆ Parents – love, respect, emotional support, listening, extent of their support to help you achieve your goals.

◆ Teammates – friendship, assistance in improving play.

◆ Media – opportunity to be yourself, chance to respond to questions when interviewed.

In reviewing these examples, be sure to realize that you may have other positive and valuable things you desire from these people or other people. If so, make sure you not only understand what these things are, but also how they will contribute to quality interpersonal relationships with these people.

Specify needs and interests of the other people

Specify the needs and interests of the other people with whom you want to maintain quality interpersonal relationships. A quality interpersonal relationship requires give and take between the parties. In your situation, it is also important to specify how you can benefit the other people with whom you have contact.

Several positive things are likely to happen.

Focusing your attention on the other person prevents a self-centered relationship.

1 First, you will be focusing your attention on the other person, thereby helping to prevent a self-centered relationship.

2 Second, you can focus your attention on the person and determine what you need to give to them as part of the relationship. In this way, a quality relationship is likely to result between you and others.

Typically, this approach may come across as too direct and impersonal—perhaps even threatening to an individual. Since interpersonal relationships usually develop in more informal, subtle, and even sensitive ways, you can try to determine what it seems the other person would like and that you can provide those things.

Steer the relationship in a positive direction

One way that you specify the needs and interests of others in terms of your relationships with them is to just ask each person what they expect and what they want from the relationship.

You can help steer the relationship in a positive direction. Essentially, you can obtain important information from conversations with them and your observations of the developing relationship. Further, the following questions may help focus your attention:

◆ What can I provide this person in exchange for what they have given me?

◆ How might what I give be important to this person?

What can you give?

Here are some general things you can give to people that will be appreciated in general by anyone:

◆ Respect for the person as someone who is unique and special.

You will receive verbal feedback and written feedback.

Some personal feedback that you will receive will be expected; other feedback to you may come that you did not expect.

The way you accept personal feedback from other people will influence your future performance and the quality of your interpersonal relationships.

Some of the feedback that you will receive will come from people when they speak directly to you. This is known as verbal feedback. For example, if your coach tells you that he does not think you were prepared mentally for a match that was just concluded in which you lost, you are being provided verbal feedback on a particular aspect of a specific performance.

Other feedback that you will get will come to you in written form like a college coach's review of your qualifications for a tennis scholarship to their university, or statistics about the percentage of first serves you made in a match in the last tournament.

Be ready for feedback

Some personal feedback that you will receive will be expected; other feedback may come that you did not expect.

The way you accept personal feedback from other people will greatly influence your future performance and the quality of your interpersonal relationships.

If you are told by your coach, for instance, that you can benefit by improving your focus and concentration on the court, you can take the feedback as intended to help you improve; then you can take personal actions to work on the need.

Using this approach, you are likely to continue an open communication with your coach.

If you become angry and upset with the coach and yourself about that feedback, the chances are that no one will benefit. Then the quality of your interpersonal relationship with the coach will decrease.

Develop a positive and respectful attitude toward feedback

We suggest, therefore, that you accept ALL feedback on yourself in a positive way.

Although you may not use the information, and even if you do not necessarily agree with it, you can still be positive and respectful of whomever provides the feedback to you. And, you can take or leave the feedback for what it's worth depending on the source and validity of the input. In this way, you will remain composed and you will set the conditions for development and continuation of a quality relationship with the other person.

Situations and suggestions for accepting feedback

Below are four situations and suggestions for accepting feedback on yourself from other people in a positive way. This involves:

◆ Understanding the kinds of personal feedback that you can receive

◆ Considering the particular personal feedback that you are being provided by another person, be that individual a coach, friend, or parent. Then, decide what it best means to you and what you can do with the information

It is helpful for you to consider four distinct feedback situations that you are likely to experience as you develop as a tennis player and as you go about becoming mentally efficient with respect to your game.

In each situation, a certain kind of feedback is provided to you that means something specific for you in terms of your subsequent actions.

The four situations we would like you to consider are as follows:

Situation 1

Feedback can be positive and expected.

In this type of personal feedback situation, you are being told something about your performance or progress—or receiving something in writing about it—that you consider to be positive and expected.

For example, this may be feedback from a coach that your overall serve and volley game is developing nicely. This feedback essentially means that you should continue to do what you have been doing and to keep practicing to improve even further.

Situation 2

Feedback can be positive and unexpected.

In this situation, you receive verbal or written feedback about your court performance or overall tennis development that is positive but unexpected.

If you were surprised to be told by your coach, for instance, that you have the ability to play at the next level of competition, this represents a "pleasant surprise." In reacting to this, you want to keep doing the things you have been doing, but you may want to get a better idea of what the person providing you with the feedback means by their statement and why they made it to you at that particular time.

Situation 3

Feedback can be negative and expected.

In this situation, the feedback can best be considered as negative and expected. It indicates that you are not doing as well as desired or anticipated, but you are aware of the situation. It is your responsibility to confront the situation and do something positive about it.

Situation 4

Feedback can be negative and unexpected.

This situation and its meaning for action is similar to the third situation, except that the feedback is negative and unexpected. In this situation, you are likely to be surprised and disappointed. However, you should still accept this in as positive a manner as possible and confront the situation head on and constructively.

Clarify what the person means

Make sure you are clear on the feedback no matter what type it is.

No matter what type of feedback you receive, you need to make sure that you understand and have clarified exactly what the person means by it. If it is very clear to you what they are saying, you may not need to ask questions about it. If the feedback is not clear in any way, and you do not know what the other person means by it (e.g., saying that you are not "playing well"), ask that individual to be more specific. Have them detail to you what they mean or give you examples to illustrate their points.

Listen to the person

Be a good listener.

When the person from whom you are receiving feedback gives you more detailed information, explanations, or reasons, it is important for you to listen to them. If necessary, ask them to give you more examples or other information. Make sure to thank them for their assistance and their helpfulness to you.

Use the feedback

Decide how specifically you can use the personal feedback to improve your performance as a tennis player and as a unique individual who exists beyond the tennis court.

4. Provide personal feedback constructively.

To maintain quality interpersonal relationships, it will be necessary for you to give feedback to other people.

To maintain quality interpersonal relationships, it will be necessary for you to give feedback to other people. Usually this feedback will be verbal.

Other feedback may be in written form, depending on the person to whom you're providing information.

Follow the Golden Rule

Do unto others as you would have them do unto you.

To give feedback to others constructively, we recommend that you abide by the old saying, "Do unto others as you would have them do unto you." You can rely on the guidelines listed below to give constructive feedback to other people:

Guideline 1

Clarify with the individual why you are providing feedback. Also, tell the person how you hope the feedback will be helpful to them.

Guideline 2

Be specific and clear when providing feedback.

When providing feedback to the person, be as specific and clear as possible in what you mean by the words you are saying and the value judgments that you might be making (e.g., feedback to your coach that he/she seems to always be criticizing you).

Guideline 3

Look for nonverbal signs.

Listen to how the person reacts to what you have said to them. Look for any nonverbal signs such as a defensive posture (e.g., hands folded across chest) that might indicate the person does not like what you have told them. Try to understand what their concerns are and attempt to address those concerns as well as you can (e.g., your coaches may really be unaware until now that they have been criticizing you quite a bit).

Guideline 4

Provide additional information to the person.

If it is requested, provide additional information to the person, assuming that it is available (e.g., to give the coach examples of their criticism). If information that a person wants from you is not available, you should make every attempt to provide this information even if you have to obtain it from somewhere else. In this case, you can set up another time with the person to discuss it further.

5. Manage interpersonal conflict effectively.

Conflict is likely to occur at some point in any interpersonal relationship. However, conflict does not have to be negative. In most cases, conflict becomes unpleasant for the parties involved because of how it is perceived by them and how each individual tries to resolve it.

In many instances, conflict is handled ineffectively, and a deteriorating interpersonal relationship is the result. Therefore, the quality of the relationship is diminished. You can consider various things in managing conflict with any other individual, a coach, parent, or friend.

Conflict reflects a difference of opinion

A conflict situation reflects a difference of opinion between two people. An example would be a difference between you and a coach. This difference of opinion is either about a means to do something, like how to play a specific opponent, or about some goals such as whether you are ready to play in a certain competitive event.

Means vs. ends

Conflicts between individuals often develop because the individuals involved are not aware of whether they are disagreeing over means or ends. For example, means have to do with the *way* a tennis match is played, or the *way* a practice is conducted. Ends have to do with the *outcome* of the match or the *quality* of practice.

Because the parties involved do not have a clear understanding of this and do not agree about what is at stake, it is difficult to proceed to resolve the conflict effectively. This is so because no one has taken the time to focus on what the conflict is really about.

When conflict occurs in an interpersonal relationship, try to manage it effectively.

Conflicts between individuals often develop because the individuals involved are not aware of whether they are disagreeing over means or ends.

Conflict is a growth situation

In addition to understanding the conflict, it is useful to have a good, positive appreciation for interpersonal conflict. A conflict situation can be a positive experience and a growth situation for the people involved.

A conflict situation can be a positive experience and a growth situation for the people involved.

When two individuals, such as you and a coach, really work at understanding a conflict situation, and when both of you try to resolve it, the situation can help both of you learn how to work together more effectively in the future, including managing further interpersonal conflict.

Conflict occurs in any setting

Interpersonal disagreement can happen in any setting— on the tennis court, at school, at home, at work, and so forth. The task of managing interpersonal conflict will best occur when it is seen as the responsibility of both parties.

Interpersonal disagreement can happen in any setting.

Guidelines to prevent and resolve conflict

Here are some guidelines that are useful in preventing and resolving an interpersonal conflict:

Guideline 1

Specify the individuals who are involved in a difference of opinion. For example, the individuals may be you and your tennis coach.

Guideline 2

Once you have specified these individuals, determine exactly what the difference of opinion is about. Is the difference of opinion about a *means* to an end such as game strategy, technique, or physical skill development; or is it about the *end* itself, such as your place on a team, or what you are expected to accomplish in terms of training or tournament play?

First discuss the areas that you agree on, then those areas you disagree on.

Guideline 3

When the precise difference of opinion is specified by you and the other person (e.g., your tennis coach), focus your attention on the factor that is in dispute (e.g., practicing a certain type of drill). First discuss the areas that you have in agreement, then those areas that you might disagree on (e.g., the length of time to accomplish the drill).

Guideline 4

When the area of disagreement has been determined, discuss how you can reach an agreement that is mutually acceptable to both of you—a compromise (e.g., a trial period for the drill).

Discuss how you can reach an agreement that is mutually acceptable to both of you.

Guideline 5

Restate the compromise as a personal action that you will take to enhance your performance and to maintain a trusting relationship with the other person (e.g., "I will participate in the drill in a quality and all-out way.")

Guideline 6

Follow through on this personal action, with the support of the other individual. Monitor the results, and make any necessary revisions.

Restate the compromise as a personal action.

In taking this kind of a mature approach to managing conflict, your focus of attention is on something that is tangible. The action that you need to take as a compromise or solution to the conflict situation can be monitored objectively with data and the support of others. This approach will also help make you a more mentally efficient player.

Follow through on this personal action.

You need quality interpersonal relationships in tennis and in the other areas of your life.

CHAPTER SUMMARY

In this chapter, we focused on how to establish and maintain quality interpersonal relationships both on and off the tennis court. We recognized the need for quality interpersonal relationships in tennis and in the other areas of your life and discussed the personal benefits to be gained and problems that can be prevented by maintaining the quality of your interpersonal relationships.

Then we presented Step 5 of the Mental Efficiency Program: Make your contacts with people quality experiences. For this step, we discussed and illustrated its associated activities:

◆ Identify your personal network.

◆ Take the lead in relating to others.

◆ Accept personal feedback positively.

◆ Provide personal feedback constructively.

◆ Manage interpersonal conflict effectively.

7

DEVELOPING

POSITIVE

SELF-ESTEEM

Nick and Arthur Ashe in front of the new Academy on 34th Street in Bradenton— World Headquarters for the NBTA today.

Even the knowledge of my own fallibility cannot keep me from making mistakes. Only when I fall do I get up again.

Vincent van Gogh
Dutch Painter

I have not failed, I have discovered 1200 materials that wouldn't work.

Thomas Edison
American Inventor

It's very, very dangerous to have your self-worth riding on your results as an athlete.

Jim Courier
Tennis Player

In a sense, this chapter is really about Arthur Ashe.

There are very few people that I remember—or want to—because I'm not really overly impressed by people per se. What I am impressed with is what someone has done—someone who reaches their best at what they do, whatever it is.

I am also impressed by what people come through under the most adverse conditions in life. There is a quote that I give out in my speeches and clinics to children and parents: "I judge people not when everything is going right, but when everything seems to be going wrong."

Arthur Ashe is one of the few people who fit pre-

cisely into this distinct category. His life and his tennis are an inspiration. I still do not fathom how he was able to do it—not being able to participate in tournaments, practice sessions, join a tennis club, even go to the bathroom or change clothes because of his skin color. This still tears at me.

And then to win the U.S. Open, to be number one in the world, to be the inspiration for his people and a model for all in sport and out as a black man. I am amazed. I feel blessed that I was able to know and work with Arthur Ashe.

As his career developed and moved beyond the game of tennis, the impact of Arthur Ashe was unheralded not only in the sports world, but in every walk of life from politics and world leaders to media to Madison Avenue and Hollywood to the common man, including politicians.

His life continues in the lives and struggles of those, who like him, were oppressed, disenfranchised, wronged, or had their rights or freedom withheld. Their fight was his—and his fight was theirs.

Then he was faced with a fight that even he could not defeat—how sad.

Arthur Ashe never would accept that life had to be unfair or unjust. Rather, he found it as another challenge that he would—in his own quiet and methodical way—work to right.

When he found out he had AIDS, he faced it head on. He redoubled his efforts in other areas. He fought harder and faster because he knew his time was limited. For Ashe, facing death was simply another challenge of life.

Perhaps his identifiability with the disease was in a master plan by God to bring Ashe's name, persona, and resources to the front in the fight against it. Ashe went right to work and accepted his circumstance as a vehicle to help combat the disease. The exposure that he and a few other prominent figures have brought to the AIDS fight—and the fact that Arthur was an innocent victim in contracting it—have been phenomenal.

When I believe that I have been wronged, I think about how Arthur might have handled the situation. The natural tendency is to react (I'm great at that), rather than back off and reflect.

Arthur was one of a kind. His story is one that will live long after Arthur Ashe, the person. He will live on through the deeds and efforts of his wonderful wife, Jeanne, and the sparkle and life in his little daughter, Camera. His name will always be associated with the loftiest of ideals, humanity, and spirit—so rare today. He will be remembered after kings, presidents, world leaders, and movie idols are all gone. We say he was good for sport, for life. Selfishly, I know that he was good for me— a champion in so many ways other than the game that brought us together—and that I am a better person in having known him.

Nick Bollettieri

7 | DEVELOPING POSITIVE SELF-ESTEEM

WHAT'S IN THIS CHAPTER

Self-esteem means what you think about yourself and how you judge yourself as an individual.

In this chapter, we discuss you and how you think and feel about yourself—the esteem, or regard, that you have for yourself. We also suggest to you methods of developing and improving your self-esteem on the court and off and in other areas of your life.

Self-esteem means what you think about yourself and how you judge yourself as an individual. It is important for you to think highly of yourself in everything you do, no matter how you perform as a tennis player or in other endeavors.

WHY YOU NEED SELF-ESTEEM

Positive self-esteem is essential to your development and mental efficiency as a tennis player and person. Without positive self-esteem—the ability to feel good about yourself—life can be very unsatisfactory and even painful.

You can think about yourself either positively or negatively.

Because each individual has the capacity to think about themselves, you can think about yourself either positively or negatively. For example, when you take pride in your training before an important match and compliment yourself on your quality practice sessions, you are thinking positively and placing yourself in a positive light. This is the situation, regardless of whether you win or lose the match.

159

If, however, you equate the loss of a match with your value as a person, you are making a negative judgment about yourself. In the first example above, you are likely to maintain positive self-esteem. In the second, your worth in regard to your tennis ability is likely to contribute to negative self-esteem.

JUDGING YOURSELF

Judging yourself by things over which you have no control is setting yourself up for a negative situation.

The need for positive self-esteem and the ability to maintain a positive self-esteem has to do with your capacity for thought and your ability to make judgments about yourself as a worthwhile person. This personal quality, in turn, contributes to your mental efficiency as a tennis player.

It is one thing to like or dislike external factors that may affect play—playing surface conditions, the wind, the sun, the attitude of your opponent, etc. These are factors about which you have no control. However, when you make judgments about yourself based on these external factors, and you reject parts of yourself (e.g., worth as a person) in the process, you set the conditions for dissatisfaction, hurt, and personal helplessness.

This causes considerable emotional pain and limits your ability and willingness to enjoy playing tennis, meeting other people, and living life to the fullest. It affects whether you are happy or not.

EACH OF US IS UNIQUE

You need to know and believe that you are a unique individual.

In considering your self-esteem, you need to know and believe that you are a unique individual. In doing so, it is very important to make sure that you do not equate the level of your tennis performance with your value as a person.

Thinking poorly about yourself can cause you to develop further negative thoughts, judgments, and painful feelings about yourself. This may cause your actions to become negative, and a self-fulfilling prophecy of poor self-esteem is the result.

GAIN PERSONAL BENEFITS

There are several personal benefits if you develop and maintain positive self-esteem.

1 First, you will enjoy yourself more when you make a conscious decision to trust yourself with personal respect and dignity. When you do this, you will be able to separate the quality of your performance—day in and day out—from your overall worth as a person. Therefore, when you have a bad day on the court, you will not conclude that you are a bad person.

2 A second major benefit of positive self-esteem is the high regard that you will develop and hold for yourself. This will enable you to view all aspects of your life as positive events, as learning experiences, and as personal challenges. As a result, the likelihood is increased that you will focus on recognizing opportunities for your personal growth and development. You will not fear failure at anything, because to fail in a task does not mean you are a poor person.

PREVENT PROBLEMS

By possessing positive self-esteem, you will be able to prevent particular self-defeating and negative personal conditions from developing. As a result, you will be more mentally efficient as a tennis player and overall individual.

1 First, you will be able to counter and eliminate negative ways of viewing activities in your life. For example, if you lose a match to an opponent you felt you should have beaten, you can focus on the facts as to why your performance was not effective—not being prepared sufficiently, getting distracted during the match by other things, and so forth. If so, you then can decide that you will learn from this experience for future performances.

You will be able to separate the quality of your performance from your overall worth as a person.

You will be able to counter and eliminate negative ways of viewing activities in your life.

You can prevent developing a poor opinion of yourself – devaluing yourself as an individual.

2 A second problem you can prevent is developing a poor opinion of yourself—devaluing yourself as an individual. This kind of personal devaluation has been identified as contributing to feelings of hopelessness in athletes and others who choose not to perform well or not to lead a quality existence on a day-to-day basis.

Step 6

Regard yourself as a unique individual.

You can engage in several activities that will allow you to treat yourself as a unique and positive person. Making sure you are following through on these activities will contribute to your positive self-esteem. These activities are:

Practice and follow through on activities that will develop and maintain your self-esteem.

1. Influence yourself beyond tennis.

2. Dispute and displace irrational beliefs.

3. Foster positive self-talk.

4. Deal with your mistakes.

5. Accept yourself as valuable and worthwhile.

These activities will be discussed in the remainder of this chapter.

1. Influence yourself beyond tennis.

The true value that you possess for your life does not come from playing tennis.

The true value that you possess for your life does not come from playing tennis. Rather, your worth as a unique individual comes from you, yourself, beyond that sport or any activity in your life. When you seek to develop and improve your self-esteem, the first place to look is at yourself in an objective, real, and broad-based way. This also means looking at yourself in the here and now; not the past nor the future.

Following are some guidelines for influencing yourself beyond the sport of tennis.

It is difficult for any individual, including you, to have an accurate idea of physical appearance, let alone other personal traits and dispositions. If we expect to receive positive feedback, we need to give positive feedback to others. As we discussed in the chapter on developing quality interpersonal relationships—"doing unto others as you would want them to do unto you" is a way to enhance and increase your self-esteem as well as to remain a mentally efficient tennis player and individual.

It is important for you to engage in a wide variety of activities beyond tennis.

Engage in a wide variety of activities

It is important for you to engage in a wide variety of activities beyond tennis. This will allow a negative experience in one area to not distort your view of yourself or your self-esteem in another.

If you are able to view yourself in a wide variety of settings like in school, in the community, and in your family, then when things are not going well in one area, you do not have to feel that it would affect you in other areas of your life.

It is important that you use yourself, not others, as a basis for comparison.

At any one time, you will be doing well in some areas. Consequently, you will not be one-dimensional, especially with regard to playing tennis.

Control feelings of envy

You must make sure to control feelings of envy. While you strive to improve your tennis game and all other areas of your life, it is important that you use yourself, not others, as a basis for comparison.

It is important to be satisfied with small, but steady gains and improvements in all that you do.

It is important to be satisfied with small, but steady gains and improvements in all that you do. Do not look for the "easy, quick fix." There is no such thing—no easy road—you get what you pay for.

While role models in tennis and the world of work are important for you—which we will discuss in more detail in

Look at yourself accurately and positively

Make a determination to look at yourself in an accurate way and in a positive manner. It is important that you are aware of your personal strong points, limitations, and need for development. Chapter 2 focuses in detail on this area how to really know yourself. In this current chapter, too, want to emphasize that personal awareness is a very basic step in learning from an experience, determining who you are, and making sure that you are more than just a tennis player.

Make a determination to look at yourself in an accurate, positive way.

It is important to have an accurate view of what you can and cannot do. Commit yourself to being positive and look for ways to improve yourself. Make sure that this positive view is balanced and realistic—not too far beyond your capabilities at any particular time.

It is important to have an accurate view of what you can and cannot do.

Be realistic in what you attempt to do

Be realistic in what you attempt to do. At times, you will discouraged—either on the tennis court or off it—and you may react by trying to make too many changes at one time. This approach usually does not work and can actually cause you to continue to get frustrated, upset, and then stop altogether. Trying to do too much in too short a time can result developing negative feelings about yourself, with lowered self-esteem.

Be realistic in what you attempt to do.

Clearly, we all should seek ways to improve our tennis game, scholastic performance, and other things that we do. But, we need to be realistic and seek to improve slowly and continually, one step at a time.

Enjoy positive interactions with people

Usually, the way we make judgments about who we are comes from what people tell us about ourselves. This includes coaches, parents, teachers, tennis opponents, friends, and other people.

Usually, the way we make judgments about who we are comes from what people tell us about ourselves.

the chapter on continuous improvement—do not look for role models who have more money, more skill, or more opportunities than you. Instead, focus on yourself and the challenge of seeing yourself get better each and every day.

Be yourself

Be yourself. By doing this, we encourage you to trust yourself, your instincts, and inclinations.

2. Dispute and displace irrational beliefs.

You will be at risk for lowering your self-esteem if you maintain or create certain beliefs about yourself that are irrational.

You will be at risk for lowering your self-esteem if you maintain or create certain beliefs about yourself that are irrational. For example, if you were to believe that all people with whom you come into contact in your tennis career must like you, then you will have placed yourself at risk for lowered self-esteem.

This is because the belief is basically irrational—it cannot possibly come true all of the time.

Beliefs that you may have about yourself in the area of tennis and beyond that are irrational because they are not possible will result in self-defeating beliefs that put you at risk for lowered self-esteem. You have to be able to "let them go" from your mind. (How to do this will be explained shortly.)

You have to be able to let go of the self-defeating beliefs.

Irrational beliefs

All these irrational beliefs, including those illustrated below, have two words in them: "should" and "must." These particular words are at the basis of the beliefs. The words communicate the message that things are demanded, there is only one way, and that there are not other alternatives to take in a situation.

Below are some beliefs and comments about why they are irrational and how they can lower your self-esteem.

You can be confident about being able to perform well, while recognizing that you will never be perfect.

Being completely competent

"I must be completely competent as a tennis player and not make any mechanical mistakes." No one person can execute flawlessly at anything, especially a complex, action-oriented sport like tennis. It is impossible to say that you should be competent all the time in all areas of your tennis, or in any other area of your life. You can be confident about being able to perform well, while recognizing that you will never be perfect. Chapter 4, on self-confidence, describes how you can keep this rational balance.

Knowing and foreseeing everything

"I must know and foresee everything." In tennis, making quick adjustments as you proceed during play is inevitable. However, the reality is that no one—including yourself or your coach—can foresee what will happen as he or she plays.

It is not possible to predict how you will perform, and it makes no sense to believe that you will always know exactly how you'll do. This irrational belief, therefore, is best not to be part of your belief system. Rather, just enjoy the process of playing tennis and the challenge of getting better with each practice or match.

It is important to recognize your anxiety, accept it, and take steps to reduce it.

Never being afraid

"I must never be afraid." Fear of the unknown is natural. Anxiety before a match and during games is expected. To believe that being afraid will not happen is not being realistic. The important thing is to recognize your anxiety, accept it, and take steps to reduce it through such vehicles as use of positive imagery (visualization) coupled with relaxation. In particular, these methods are discussed in Chapter 3 on achieving self-motivation and Chapter 5 on self-discipline.

Being totally reliant on myself

"I don't need anyone or help from anyone. I'll do it myself."

This kind of belief is self-defeating and damaging to self-esteem because a person must receive support from a range of people to be successful and to possess good self-esteem.

Dispute and displace irrational beliefs.

Procedures to defeat irrational thoughts

The important thing for you is not to let these kinds of thoughts influence you but rather to dispute them and displace them.

Listed below are some procedures to follow.

Identify any irrational beliefs

Identify any irrational beliefs—such as the kinds described above—that you may have and that you believe have affected your on court tennis performance or your overall development.

Identify any irrational beliefs.

In identifying these irrational beliefs, determine as precisely as possible the following things as they pertain to you:

◆ When each irrational belief occurs (e.g., prior to the match while warming up; between serves; at home).

◆ The feelings you experience when you think about the belief (e.g., fear, worry, doubt, sadness).

◆ What you do immediately after having the irrational belief and feelings (e.g., become distracted; lose interest in the practice session).

Personal awareness of your beliefs can help you dispel them.

You need to make these determinations so that you can become aware about your thoughts, feelings, and actions in relation to any one belief. Personal awareness of your beliefs can help you dispel them.

Dispute each belief

Once you have identified each irrational belief, described each one, and developed an understanding of it, you now are in position to dispute the belief. To dispute an irrational belief, do the following:

◆ State the belief to yourself, or read it if you have written it down.

◆ Challenge yourself to prove that this belief is accurate and possible. Ask yourself what evidence there is that can actually make it real.

◆ Question the belief in terms of your goals—ask yourself whether this kind of irrational belief is going to stand in the way of your effective performance on the court and your long-term development as a tennis player.

◆ Encourage yourself to now rise above the irrational belief—recognizing it for what it is—false.

Substitute rational beliefs

Substitute more appropriate beliefs and perspectives for each irrational belief that you now have disputed. Create for yourself and monitor more appropriate beliefs and perspectives. Monitoring your beliefs will help discourage any relapses.

3. Foster positive self-talk.

All people, including tennis players, talk to themselves. However, the way you talk to yourself will affect your self-esteem. In this sense, self-talk that can be considered positive will enhance positive self-esteem.

Conversely, negative self-talk usually leads to lowered self-esteem. When you think about something, such as getting your serve into the targets you want, you are also saying things to yourself.

You usually believe what you hear

Often, these negative statements are very subtle and you are not aware of them. When you do "hear them," you are likely to believe—or pay attention to—what you say to yourself.

Positive self-talk means that you make statements that put

Substitute more appropriate beliefs and perspectives for each irrational belief that you now have disputed.

Negative self-talk usually leads to lowered self-esteem.

Positive self-talk means that you make statements that put yourself in a favorable light and perspective.

yourself in a favorable light and perspective—you create self-esteem. For example, when you say something like "Just take one point at a time —relax and hit the ball," you are talking to yourself in a positive way.

In contrast, if you made a statement to yourself such as, "I'll never beat my opponent—what will everyone think?", you are using negative self-talk. If you routinely employ positive self-talk, you are likely to be positive about yourself, and your self-esteem will be enhanced.

If you usually talk to yourself in negative terms, you are contributing to low self-esteem. Fortunately, you are able to foster positive self-talk. You are able to control what you say to yourself, how, and when, including changing negative self-talk to positive self-talk.

If you routinely employ positive self-talk, you are likely to be positive about yourself, and your self-esteem will be enhanced.

A basic thing you can do to foster positive self-talk is to increase the awareness of how you talk to yourself in various situations that have to do with playing tennis as well as other areas in your life.

Suggestions for positive self-talk

There are actions that you can take to foster positive self-talk. Some suggestions are listed below.

How do you talk to yourself?

Identify and list the various situations in which you examine how you talk to yourself.

Identify and list the various situations you want to consider in which you examine how you talk to yourself. With respect to tennis, these situations may be ones such as pre-match preparation, warmup time, actual match play, changeovers, and other situations.

To help you identify and list these situations, use the form in Figure 7-1, Self-Talk Assessment Form, on page 172.

For each situation you have listed on the form, describe the self-statement you made to yourself on a routine basis.

Repeat your self-statement on a routine basis

For each situation you have listed on the form, describe the self-statement you make to yourself on a routine basis. If you cannot come up with a self-statement for the situations that you have listed, then don't concern yourself with those situations. Rather, just focus on the situations that you can describe.

Differentiate the positive from the negative

Consider each self-statement you have described on the form. Indicate in the space provided whether the statement is (a) a positive self-statement, or (b) a negative self-statement.

By using this method, you will have a good idea of the positive statements that you want to keep using in the situations you have identified. You now are able to decide which positive thoughts can be substituted for the negative ones. You can record these as actions on the form.

Eliminate the negative and foster the positive

Make notes on the form of any personal actions you can take to eliminate negative self-statements and foster your use of positive self-talk.

When you are practicing or playing in matches, you can foster positive self-talk by substituting the positive for the negative.

For example, when you are practicing or playing in matches, you can foster positive self-talk by substituting the positive for the negative.

When you recognize that you are talking to yourself in a negative way, you can take a deep breath, relax, and immediately focus on a positive thought. When the same negative thought begins to emerge again, you can use a basic thought-stopping procedure to get rid of the thought.

This involves repeating the word "no" to yourself which is intended to get rid of the negative thought. Then, quickly take a deep breath, relax, and substitute a corresponding positive thought.

Figure 7-2 on page 173 is a completed version illustrating use of the Self-Talk Assessment Form.

4. Deal with your mistakes.

Sometimes, you do something that you regret. You make a mistake. It may have to do with something you've done to yourself or to another person. It may occur on the court or off the court. Often, the mistake "gets to you" and makes you feel bad. You may think poorly of yourself and downgrade yourself. As such, your self-esteem is affected.

Self-esteem, though, is not something that occurs before or after you make mistakes. Rather, self-esteem has to do with unconditional acceptance of yourself despite any mistakes you feel you may have made.

Prevent a low self-esteem

To prevent this kind of personal confusion and lowering of your self-esteem, you can take the actions listed below.

Change the perspective of the mistake

Change the perspective that you have about the mistake. Instead of viewing the event as something awful or problematic, you can reframe it to yourself as a positive learning experience.

You can seek to determine what you know now that you were not aware of before and what this new information means for your future personal actions.

The mistake is a signal

View a mistake as a signal to yourself. By this we mean a signal to get you "back on track" and to do consistently what you already know how to do.

For example, if you initially consider losing to an opponent

Self-esteem has to do with unconditional acceptance of yourself despite any mistakes you feel you may have made.

Change the perspective that you have about the mistake.

View a mistake as a signal to yourself.

Figure 7-1. Self-Talk Assessment Form

Name_____Date_____

Situation	Self-Statement	Rating (+/-)	Personal Action
Prematch preparation (home, at courts)			
Warmup			
Match Play *-when leading* *-when behind*			
Changeovers			
Postmatch			
Practice Session			
Other			

Figure 7-2. Completed Self-Talk Assessment Form

Name_ *Bob Conroy* _____Date_ *1/9* _____

Situation	Self-Statement	Rating (+/-)	Personal Action
Prematch preparation (home, at courts)	*I really like being on this tour—the people and the challenge*	*Positive (+)*	*Remember how I feel, when I get down on myself*
Warmup			
Match Play -when leading -when behind	*I will never keep my play up against my opponent—he's really good*	*Negative (-)*	*Stop this thought by saying "no" to myself. Then focus on my next point.*
Changeovers			
Postmatch			
Practice Session	*I'm tired. It's time to stop.*	*Negative (-)*	*Say this to myself: "I'll take each drill one at a time." "I'll do a quality job on each one."*
Other			

of much lesser ability as a mistake, you can choose to view it as a warning to focus on in terms of being overconfident, letting up, or being indifferent or cocky to any opponent.

Mistakes happen

Mistakes occur for everyone all the time – that's part of life.

Mistakes occur for everyone all the time—that's part of life. View mistakes as things that will happen. Sometimes, you will make them and allow for them. The important thing is not to let a fear of making a mistake, especially on the court, make you become tentative and not spontaneous in your play.

Raise awareness about mistakes

Raise your awareness about mistakes by accepting the following points for consideration:

◆ Recognize that everyone makes mistakes.

◆ Realize that you also make mistakes and will likely make them in the future.

◆ Forgive yourself for making a mistake, no matter how painful it may have been.

◆ Remember that a mistake was made at a certain point in time that has passed. You cannot recapture the mistake at this time however much you may regret having made it.

Learn from each mistake and move forward.

◆ You have already paid for the mistake in its occurrence and your reaction to it. Learn from it and move forward.

5. Accept yourself as valuable and worthwhile.

When you recognize the positive qualities that you have, without expecting perfection, you are a long way along to developing positive self-esteem and being a mentally efficient tennis player.

Accepting yourself requires an approach where you (1) consider yourself as a unique person, (2) identify your strengths, and (3) specify what you need to improve upon.

You need to accept yourself unconditionally.

Then, in an enthusiastic way, you go about accentuating the strengths and using your needs for improvement as springboards for positive personal action. What you need to do is accept yourself —unconditionally—while trying to foster positive self-talk and opinions of yourself.

CHAPTER SUMMARY

In this chapter, we discussed how to regard yourself as worthwhile and how to learn to build and maintain positive self-esteem. We identified personal benefits to be gained by regarding yourself as worthwhile and problems that can be prevented through this opinion of yourself.

Step 6 of the Mental Efficiency Program – Regard yourself as a unique individual – was presented. For this step, we discussed and illustrated the following activities:

◆ Influence yourself beyond tennis.

◆ Dispute and displace irrational beliefs.

◆ Foster positive self-talk.

◆ Deal with your mistakes.

◆ Accept yourself as valuable and worthwhile.

We now turn to the last personal quality—the ability of committing to continuous improvement.

8

COMMITTING TO CONTINUOUS IMPROVEMENT

Nick and Monica Seles at an NBTA practice session.

It ain't over till it's over.

Yogi Berra
Hall of Fame Baseball Player
New York Yankees

You try to learn from your mistakes. It's stupid to turn away from them as if they didn't happen. If you don't learn from them, they really are mistakes.

Jim Abbott
New York Yankees Pitcher

When an archer misses the mark, he turns and looks for the fault within himself. Failure to hit the bull's eye is never the fault of the target. To improve your aim — improve yourself.

Gilbert Arland

As this book goes to print and perhaps for years to come, the Monica Seles story will probably still be very much in the limelight. I can still picture her as the little girl from Yugoslavia with a racquet bigger than she was and who would keep coming at you. You punch her, she would come back for another punch. You punch her again, she is going to come in closer for another punch. She is a Rocky Marciano. She wants you to keep punching because she lives to get that last punch in.

The girl I know (and would have bet everything on) would compete and be able to come through the most adverse conditions that any athlete may have to face. The story today is whether Monica Seles will come back from what most athletes never expe-

177

rience. She says she is not ready.

Very few have had to ever experience an actual life-threatening, physical assault and then convince themselves to come back and compete again.

Does Seles want to come back? Is she unsure of herself? Is the injury an excuse for not coming back? Has she achieved enough, both financially and in winning, that she is satisfied with herself?

For me, that would be difficult to accept because I was with Monica in the most formative part of her life—from 12 to 16 years old. And I would again say that I felt that if any person could come through it, it would be Monica Seles. Whether she wants to or not is another story. It certainly points to the tragedy and damage that can be caused by one senseless, single event.

If she does come back, first of all, she has to conquer the fear. She has to face the long lapse of not competing, which is not easy.

She has to make a personal commitment to get back into shape physically and to regain her fighting spirit. The former is easy for Monica—she is one of the hardest workers we have ever trained. The latter—even for Seles who is ferociously competitive—will be the hard part after what she has been through. And, knowing Monica, she will accept nothing less than coming back to the game at the same level and the same success—at least—from which she left it.

What all this means is that it will probably require Monica to lift herself to another level. I feel sorry about all that Monica has had to suffer and only hope that the decision that she finally makes is one that she can accept and live with for the rest of her life.

But, as I said in the beginning, if anyone can do it and has the strength and determination to battle seemingly insurmountable odds, it is Monica Seles. I wish her luck!

Nick Bollettieri

8 | COMMITTING TO CONTINUOUS IMPROVEMENT

WHAT'S IN THIS CHAPTER

Continuous improvement means being personally committed to using information about your progress and performance in tennis and other areas of your life.

In this chapter, we will discuss an important—although usually overlooked—aspect of positive self-development and mental efficiency: your continuous and ongoing improvement as a tennis player and person.

Continuous improvement means being personally committed to using information about your progress and performance in tennis and other areas of your life. This information serves as the springboard or catalyst for your overall development and improvement.

This growth and development may have to do with many things such as improving your personal awareness, self-motivation, self-confidence, self-discipline, the quality of your interpersonal relationships, and your self-esteem. It is no coincidence that these are the headings of the previous chapters of the book and, more important, the basic personal qualities of positive self-development and your mental efficiency program.

WHY YOU NEED CONTINUOUS IMPROVEMENT

There is a well-known principle in the physical sciences that we believe is very applicable to your positive self-development and mental efficiency. This principle states that an object or thing that is in motion will remain in motion until acted upon by some external force. If an object or thing is at rest, it will remain in that condition until it is propelled into action or another form.

If your personal growth is in motion, it will remain in motion until acted upon by some external force. If it is at rest, it will remain at rest until acted upon.

This principle is a useful one to consider in relation to yourself as a tennis player and in other areas of your life because this is a natural tendency for all people—to want to remain in action and to be propelled forward in growth and development.

ACTION VS. COMPLACENCY

Unfortunately, however, there are individuals who get into habits and personal states where they become satisfied with themselves. They do not perceive a need to improve on how they think (mental), how they use and relate to their feelings (emotional), or how they behave and act (physical). As a result, these people become complacent. They continue to do the same things, day in and day out. They are likely to become stagnant mentally, emotionally, and physically.

When someone does not seek improvement in a planned way, they are likely to become stagnant mentally, emotion-ally, and physically.

USE IT OR LOSE IT

The phrase "Use it or lose it" reminds us that when some-one does not seek to improve himself or herself in a planned way, they are likely to lose something in terms of their men-tal, emotional, and physical development. There are other people—including you—who want to continue to grow, develop, and improve themselves.

When we have researched and observed these kinds of individuals as to how they strive for continuous improve-ment, we have found that they possess both a high level of

self-motivation, as well as a very basic stimulus that keeps them propelled toward the future in positive ways. This stimulus is information they have gathered about their progress and performance and have used in a systematic manner.

HOW TO APPROACH THE TASK

The importance of continuous improvement of yourself as a tennis player and a person demands that you approach the task in a planned, systematic way.

The importance of continuous improvement of yourse' a tennis player and a person demands that you approac task in a planned, systematic way. You need to be able commit yourself to perform well and to accept the ch to do the best job possible during practice sessions, and competitive play.

In addition, you can come to appreciate the va¹ excitement of acquiring new knowledge, skills, ⨍ if for no other reason than that these activities ⨍ acquire and that they can be used to better yc

By continuous improvement of your me' and physical skills, you will be sharp, pro maintain a competitive edge. Most impc yourself more as you change and as yo' improve your mental efficiency.

By continuous improvement of your mental, emotional, and physical skills, you will be sharp, productive, and able to maintain a competitive edge.

GAIN PERSONAL BENEFITS

You can realize several benefits continuous improvement.

1 First, you will become in' ing actions for your imr back and letting things just ' move forward—in precise tennis player and person lus through use of infor cussed later in the cha'

2 A second benefit for you involves the actual personal changes you will experience. These changes will be experienced in the following areas: (a) how you learn to refine your thinking, reasoning, and problem-solving abilities relevant to tennis, school, family, and community; (b) how you become more proficient at managing your emotions; and (c) how you acquire and improve your physical skills.

PREVENT PROBLEMS

When you commit to continuous improvement of yourself, you will also be in a strong position to prevent the development of several personal problems.

1 The first of these has to do with being complacent. This means becoming so satisfied with your current levels of performance and development and believing that you are content to stay just the way you are. When you make a decision to remain the same, chances are that you will actually regress or go backward in your development. This will occur because you are not doing anything to develop your skills or to acquire new ones.

2 The second problem that will be prevented is that of psychological helplessness. This is a condition in which an individual perceives themselves as so far behind—as so stagnant and inactive—that they view their situation as futile and beyond their control.

This type of individual becomes resigned to their particular point and place in time. They decide not to make changes for their development and usually become unhappy and even angry at themselves and life.

**ommitting to
ntinuous
rovement of
self will help
prevent a
lacent attitude
schological
sness.**

Step 7

Commit yourself to continuous improvement.

You can engage in several activities that will help you commit to continuous improvement. These activities should not, however, be used in a completely unchangeable way. Rather, they need to be adapted to your situation and circumstances. They need to be dynamic. These activities are listed below.

1. Obtain feedback.

2. Schedule meetings with yourself.

3. Take the personal initiative.

1. Obtain feedback.

Progress feedback is information that you obtain about yourself that indicates the amount of growth or improvement in your activity or activities from one point in time to another point.

You need to obtain two kinds of feedback on yourself as a basis for your continuous improvement. These types of feedback are referred to here as "progress feedback" and "performance feedback."

Progress feedback

Typically, progress feedback involves obtaining information on the extent to which you are making progress or attaining your personal goals as we discussed in the chapter on self-motivation.

Performance feedback

Performance feedback is the data that indicates the results of your play.

Performance feedback is the data that indicates the results of your play—either during practice sessions or in competitions.

How to obtain feedback

You can obtain process feedback and performance feedback on yourself by using the systematic approach detailed below.

Review your progress ratings on your personal goals

You can also review the ratings that you have made on your progress to your personal goals and the similar ratings made by your coach. These ratings will allow you to make judgments about your progress. The Personal Goals Form in Chapter 3 can be used for this purpose.

Review progress in several other areas

You need to also review your progress in several other areas in addition to your progress goals. For example, you can obtain information about the extent to which you have progressed in the area of self-confidence during match play. You can obtain this feedback by rating yourself using the following scale:

> 1 = Excellent progress
> 2 = Good amount
> 3 = Average
> 4 = Fair amount
> 5 = Poor progress

Make these ratings on a weekly basis. In addition, you can ask your coach to provide an opinion about how you are progressing in the area of self-confidence in match play. You can then can discuss your ratings with your coach. If a discrepancy exists between these two evaluations, you can discuss reasons for it and any change that you may want to make. It is possible that each of you could be viewing self-confidence in a different way.

Progress in self-discipline

You can also obtain information about the progress you are making in the area of self-discipline. You can use the same procedure and rating scale as described just above.

Progress in performance

For performance feedback purposes, you can review data

Review your goal ratings in Chapter 3.

Ask your coach to provide an opinion about how you are progressing in the area of self-confidence in match play.

on your results from match play and from practice. This data can be kept by someone helping you in your goals and/or by your coach.

Here are some examples of the types of data (results) that you can review to make judgments about your performance:

◆ Number of first serves in; number of second serves; percentage of returns

◆ Percentage of ads won; lost

◆ Percentage of break points won; lost

◆ Double faults

◆ Percentage of points won at the net

◆ Forehand passing shots attempted; executed

◆ Backhand passing shots attempted; executed

◆ First points won

Watch videotape of your play

Watching a videotape can help you compare your current performance to a previous tape.

You also can watch videotape of your play. In this way, you can make judgments about your progress in various areas relative to a previous tape as well as make judgments about your current performance.

You can watch the video alone or with your coach. If you view the tape with your coach, there will be an opportunity for the two of you to discuss your progress and performance. Here are examples of what you can watch for on a videotape.

◆ Quality of strokes, stroke mechanics

◆ Technique and execution

◆ Posture, balance, and appearance

◆ Composure

◆ Other

2. Schedule meetings with yourself.

About once a week, for about 20 minutes, you should schedule a personal review meeting *with yourself*. At this meeting, you can go over the feedback you have obtained on your progress and performance.

We suggest that you conduct this meeting in a place that is comfortable and where you will not be interrupted by anyone. Perhaps, the best place to *meet yourself* is at home. At this meeting, several items can form the agenda. Four sample items are described below.

Item 1

Discuss with yourself the things you are doing well or making progress on. Try to be as specific as you can. Focus on how you are coming along with respect to:

Discuss with yourself the things that you are doing well or making progress on.

◆ Progress toward your personal goals

◆ Self-motivation

◆ Self-confidence

◆ Self-discipline

◆ Quality and effectiveness of your match play

◆ Interpersonal relationships

◆ Self-esteem

Make notes about areas in which you want the opinion of your coach or others in your personal network.

In considering what you are doing well, you may want to make notes about areas in which you want the opinion of your coach or others in your personal network. By way of your personal meeting with yourself, you will have a record of what to discuss with that individual.

Item 2

Consider the things you need to improve. To do this, you can make judgments about the extent to which your progress has met (or not met) your expectations. In doing so, focus attention on:

Consider the things you need to improve.

◆ Particular goals in which you have not progressed as expected

◆ Self-motivation – you have not felt a desire or yearning to work toward one or more goals

◆ Self-confidence – you may have detected certain aspects of your play that you have not felt confident about

◆ Self-discipline – you detect that you have not followed through on what you have planned (e.g., prematch preparation)

◆ Technical or strategic aspects of your game

◆ Quality of interpersonal relationships

◆ Self-esteem – at times, you have thought less of yourself when you didn't perform well

List specific things from your discussion with yourself that you want to discuss with your coach.

Item 3

List specific things from your discussion with yourself that you want to discuss with your coach. When you write down things about your performance, mental skills, or physical skills, the likelihood is increased that you will have a productive interchange with your coach.

To conclude your meeting, summarize your thoughts and impressions.

Item 4

To conclude your meeting, summarize your thoughts and impressions. Here are several questions that can help you:

◆ What overall surprises did you discover about yourself?

◆ Did you find out certain things you did that were better than you thought?

◆ Did you identify things that indicated that you were not doing as well as expected?

◆ Did you learn things that you are not sure about and that you need to clarify with your coach?

◆ What areas did you uncover that require further development on your part?

◆ What trends or patterns did you find out about yourself?

Item 5

Schedule another personal meeting with yourself.

Schedule another personal meeting with yourself. Build this kind of meeting into your routine of daily living.

3. Take the personal initiative.

You can use the information that you have derived from your personal meeting to take a personal initiative for your continuous improvement.

You can use the information that you have derived from your personal meeting to take a personal initiative for your continuous improvement. This improvement will be in the area of tennis, and it can also be in other areas of your life. You can take this kind of personal initiative by answering the following questions and using the answers as a basis for moving forward:

◆ What do I need to do to continue to develop my personal awareness?

◆ What can I do to make sure I continue to grow in self-motivation?

◆ How can I continue to build my self-confidence?

◆ In what respect do I need to become better at self-discipline?

◆ What will enable me to continue to enhance my quality of interpersonal relationships?

◆ How can I continue to keep my self-esteem in positive directions?

Discuss answers with your coach

You can answer the questions by using the feedback information that you have about yourself. In addition, you may want to discuss your answers with your coach.

You can answer the above questions by using the feedback information that you have about yourself. In addition, you may want to discuss your answers with your coach. Then, you will be able to identify actions you can take that will facilitate your continuous improvement.

General actions toward continuous improvement

Although a range of specific actions will be possible for you to take, here are some general actions that may be appropriate for you personally:

◆ Continue to do what you have been doing. In this regard, keep monitoring how what you do affects your progress and performance.

◆ Acquire new physical or mental skills that will help your game.

◆ Set personal goals that are more specific, measurable, attainable, relevant, and timeframed.

◆ Follow through more precisely and carefully with your plans.

◆ Become more respectful and patient with other people.

◆ View yourself as a unique individual separate from your performance.

◆ Believe in yourself on a more consistent basis.

◆ Use various methods to learn.

A WORD OF ENCOURAGEMENT

To continue on a personal course of improvement, we encourage you to return to the other chapters in this book as needed. We further suggest that you read them again on a regular basis, perhaps once a year.

In doing so, the guidelines contained in the chapters will become second nature to you, and as a result, will allow you to be better able to use the material without really having to think about it.

You can adapt the procedures to your own style. Also, you

Acquire new physical or mental skills that will help your game.

Become more respectful and patient with other people.

Believe in yourself on a more consistent basis.

will have taken personal command of a framework for positive self-development and mental efficiency.

Chapter 9, the next one, will discuss in more detail how you can accomplish this.

CHAPTER SUMMARY

In this chapter of the book, we discussed how you can commit to continuous improvement of yourself, thereby developing yourself in positive ways and increasing your ability to be mentally efficient.

In particular, we focused on three activities to accomplish this aim:

◆ Obtain feedback.

◆ Schedule meetings with yourself.

◆ Take the personal initiative.

9

TAKING THE
MENTAL
EFFICIENCY
ADVANTAGE

Chris Evert at her peak.

You are really never playing an opponent. You are playing yourself, your own highest standards, and when you reach your limits, that is real joy.

Arthur Ashe
Tennis Player

You can always pitch better.
Sandy Koufax
Baseball Hall of Fame

All glory comes from daring to begin.
Eugene F. Ware
American Lawyer and Poet

Although Chris Evert was never my student, we are good friends, and she knows my deep respect for her. When I think of Chris, I think about THE lady of the game of tennis.

Like Arthur Ashe, Evert brought the sport of tennis a high degree of class and respect. If there is anyone in the game that so profoundly represents mental efficiency, it is Chris Evert. It was a part of her upbringing that she carried to the court and into all aspects of her life.

This is not to say that Chris Evert is devoid of emotion or does not have a personal side. On the contrary, she certainly does, but she knows how to present herself to the public and how to handle situations better than anyone I have ever seen. This extends far beyond being down match point and fighting back or getting a bad call on a crucial point. Chris has made her on court persona an example of pure discipline and control—one to be forever respected and admired. In all of sport, she epitomizes class. She is a role model for every young player who has touched a racquet over the last two decades and will continue to be into the future.

Let's talk about that a little bit. Chris's father, Jimmy Evert, was her first and most important coach. He instilled in Chris the ingredients that it took to win as well as play the game—both on the court and off. He instilled in her his family values, and they have made all the difference. Jimmy Evert was a father, a teacher, and most important, he was Chris's friend.

Was Chris Evert a great athlete? Not really. Did she move exceptionally well? No, just adequately. Was she a multiple shot maker? Again, not really. A big server? No. Volleys? Again, no. Put it all together and one has to ask, what did she have?

First of all, when Chris Evert practiced, when Chris Evert played, when Chris Evert spoke, when she represented the sport in post-match speeches, or clinics, or articles, when she won or lost, she gave 110%—her very best. You knew it and you felt it. There was never a letdown, never a frown or hung head on the court, only the intensity and the determination that makes a champion tick. At this, she was the best. Not one of the best, **but the very best.**

She always had control of herself. Certainly she had normal emotions and doubts and wanted to give in at times, but she never did. Most important, she never even indicated to you that she might or would even consider it. She was always posi-

tive toward herself and the sport. She gave back to everyone involved including her family, her community, her peers, the event owners, the agents, the sponsors, and her fans – all knew that they could count on Chris to give her all every time and in every way. How unique is this? Name one other athlete in any sport today of whom you can say the same.

Jimmy Evert gave Chris a strong and solid base not only for tennis, but also for life. He built this into her tennis practice, her competition, her studies, and every aspect of her growing up. Her demeanor was not found, it was practiced and perfected the same as her forehand or backhand. Her ability to be mentally effective and efficient was part of her everyday upbringing and in being so, became part of her life—part of what Chris Evert is.

I can imagine that it went like this... Jimmy whispered to Chris every day and she listened very well. "You will hit one more ball over the net than your opponent. You will hit the ball to a certain place—where your opponent is not. You will take advantage of what you can do and remember what you can't do. You will always play fair and by the rules or you won't play at all. You will treat the sport and your opponents—regardless of who they are and the circumstance you are in—with respect. Tennis is a privilege for you and all who play; not a right. You will always give your best. You will have fun. And, Chris, if you can put all this together and work hard, you will be number one in the world and be admired by all who compete—you will be the symbol for all who play and believe that they too can be a champion. This will be your philosophy both on and off the court."

Nick Bollettieri

9 | TAKING THE MENTAL EFFICIENCY ADVANTAGE

WHAT'S IN THIS CHAPTER

In this final chapter, we challenge and encourage you to take advantage of the Mental Efficiency Program. Use the information you have experienced in the book, continuously and positively, to become and remain a mentally efficient tennis player and person. In doing so, you will be taking the mental efficiency advantage and a giant step toward positive self-development in tennis, sport, and life.

CHALLENGE AND COMMIT YOURSELF

Your commitment to take the mental efficiency advantage can start right now.

The Mental Efficiency Program that has been introduced to you in this book is a program personally designed for you.

It is a program that you will implement and track your own improvement. It is a program that is dynamic—changing with your growth and needs. Most important, it is a program that will benefit you both on and off the tennis court!

Although you have now read through the book and begun your mental efficiency training, it is important to continue to take advantage of the Mental Efficiency Program by making it part of your on- and off-court life.

Becoming self-sufficient and developing your abilities and self-confidence to the highest attainable level are goals that you want to make your top priorities. Do not delay doing this. Take the mental efficiency advantage!

The steps and activities of the Mental Efficiency Program are most beneficial for you when you make them part of your daily routines—both on and off the court.

To do this, you must make a commitment to yourself to learn more about the steps and activities that make up the program. In this way, you will be applying mental efficiency effectively to your tennis training and other aspects of your life.

Your commitment to take the mental efficiency advantage has already begun. Now, by reading back through the previous eight chapters of the book, your level of commitment and knowledge of mental efficiency will increase and become more effective for you.

SET UP A SCHEDULE FOR YOURSELF

You should review and study each chapter over a prescribed period of time. For example, you can complete one chapter each day over eight consecutive days, a chapter every other day, or some other sequence that works best for you. The most important part of this is to be consistent and dedicated to your progress and improvement by using this kind of self-maintenance approach.

For each chapter, make sure you have a good understanding of the material. The better you understand the steps and activities of the Mental Efficiency Program, the more effective it will be for you and the faster you will be able to achieve the results you have set for yourself.

GUIDELINES FOR STUDY

Here are some guidelines that will help you learn quickly and effectively, and help you have fun doing so along the way to being a mentally efficient player and person:

◆ As you read each chapter again, have a note pad and

The Mental Efficiency Program is most beneficial for you when you make it part of your daily routines both on and off the court.

Set up a schedule of review and study for yourself.

pen available; or highlighter. When you come to a point in each chapter that you want to remember because it is important to you, make notes or mark the sections. In addition, add your own personal thoughts and comments.

Remember that the program is dynamic and that as you change and progress, there may be certain aspects of the Mental Efficiency Program that will become more, or less, important to you. You may need to mark new information as this occurs.

Ask the opinions of your coach, parents, and others who are interested in your improvement.

◆ Make sure to complete all of the forms in the chapters if you have not already done so. Use the information from them as described in each chapter. If you need more forms, they are available for you (call the NBTA at 813-755-1000; ask for the Mental Efficiency Department or the Pro Shop).

◆ Discuss the material you are reviewing and studying with your coach, parents, and others who are interested in your improvement and who are part of your support team—those who want you to be the best tennis player and person possible.

Mental efficiency can also be considered from a group perspective.

◆ Ask the opinions and comments of these people, including their constructive criticism, about the personal qualities, abilities, steps, and activities contained in each chapter. Remember that the Mental Efficiency Program is one that benefits both you and the members of your support team.

MENTAL EFFICIENCY: THE GROUP PERSPECTIVE

In general, this book has focused on mental efficiency and you, as an individual tennis player and person. Chapter 1 describes in detail how such a personal perspective is the foundation for your mental efficiency, performance, and development.

Mental efficiency, however, can also be considered from a group perspective. While a group treatment of mental efficiency is really a topic for an entire book, we want to provide you with some general information and some comments about it here.

WHAT IS A GROUP?

The dictionary defines a group as two or more people who come together to pursue a common purpose. In tennis, you are part of a group if you play doubles or if you are a member of a high school or college team, association, or club. A student-teacher relationship also is a group.

Regardless of the size or number of members of a group, the participants in the group are expected to coordinate their physical efforts, their common emotions, their goals, and their mental skills.

Regardless of the size or number of members of a group, the participants in the group are expected to coordinate their physical efforts, their common emotions, their goals, and their mental skills. They need to do this in order to perform well together.

In doing so, the group has the greatest opportunity to perform their skills to the best of their capabilities, win matches, improve their abilities, achieve their ranking goals, advance in tournament play, and fully enjoy the sport and their improvement in it. Were this not to be the case, the group would not be as efficient or effective.

A group effort is much like a well-running engine. When all the parts are finely tuned and working in synchronization, they run smoothly and achieve the best performance. If any of the parts are functioning poorly or ineffectively, the machine cannot reach maximum performance.

FROM THE GROUP PERSPECTIVE

When mental efficiency is considered in a group environment—in whatever group context (doubles partners or team)—very similar qualities apply to the group's mental efficiency as is applicable and witnessed at the individual level.

What differs, however, is the perspective that one takes on a specific task or setting a specific goal. In a group circumstance, the perspective is with a collection of individuals who have concerns and tasks that are common, but not individual.

In terms of group mental efficiency for tennis, sport, and life, the following qualities are important:

◆ Awareness of the members of the group (e.g., doubles, tennis team, coach/student) about its collective strengths, limitations, and needs.

◆ Motivation exhibited by members of the group to work together as a unit to attain their common group goals.

◆ Confidence that is shared by members of the group with respect to how they can perform well during competition.

◆ Discipline to work together as a unit in order to persist and persevere with the implementation of their common game plans.

◆ Relating to all members of the group—both with one another and to individuals outside the group itself—in quality ways.

◆ Establishing a regard and respect for each member of the group as worthwhile—both as an individual and as a member of the team—over and above their particular tennis ability.

◆ Improvement as a doubles pair or tennis/club team on a continuous basis.

AWARENESS OF THE GROUP

This quality has to do with the extent to which the group can assess and coordinate itself as a collective unit. In this regard, a tennis group that is mentally efficient is able to identify its collective strong points, limitations, and developmental needs.

For example, you may be part of a tennis team where the

> **A tennis group that is mentally efficient is able to identify its collective strong points, limitations, and developmental needs.**

members are noted for their aggressive serve and volley style of play as well as for their strong practice work ethic.

This particular team, however, may be limited in that they have lost their last three matches and have lost confidence in their particular style of play. They have become tentative in coming to the net for fear of losing again.

To perform well, a group also needs to commit itself to actively pursuing its common purpose.

The team may need to consider how they can best regain their confidence in the near term and perhaps develop a more "all court" style of match play to enhance their capabilities in the long term.

If the group can function in this way, it has exhibited an important quality of group mental efficiency.

GROUP MOTIVATION

To perform well, a group also needs to commit itself to actively pursuing its common purpose. For doubles partners or a tennis team to do this, however, each of the members on the team must be motivated as a unit, not simply as individuals.

Each of the group members, including you, needs to discuss with one another the setting of group goals.

This means that each of the group members, including you, needs to discuss with one another the setting of group goals. These goals are very similar to individual goals. They reflect things like working together in a quality way during practice or developing specific tactics and strategies against certain teams of individual doubles pairs.

The group must also decide to pursue these goals in an open way, making sure that there is an ongoing communication with all members of the unit. When the group makes these kinds of commitments together, they are functioning in a mentally efficient way.

CONFIDENCE OF THE GROUP

The individuals who make up the group (doubles, tennis team) have a common belief that they can perform well as a unit and accomplish their established group goals.

The individuals who make up the group (doubles, tennis team) have a common belief that they can perform well as a unit and accomplish their established group goals.

For instance, even though a tennis team has never before reached the final round of regional tournament play, the members of that group know that they have prepared themselves effectively for the forthcoming matches and have confidence in their abilities regardless of the odds. The team believes it has a good chance to win and is functioning as a mentally efficient group in terms of group confidence.

GROUP DISCIPLINE

Discipline in a group context refers to the extent to which the group can formulate a coordinated game plan – a team plan – that is over and above any individual plan and has the ability to follow through on it during competition.

Discipline in a group context refers to the extent to which the group can formulate a coordinated game plan—a team plan—that is over and above any individual plan and has the ability to follow through on it during competition.

As a quality of mental efficiency, group discipline also has to do with the extent to which the members of a group prepare themselves through rigorous practice sessions, sport specific training, and skill work to be ready to play and implement their group game plan.

For example, a tennis team may have a plan to win all of the doubles matches to gain a firm point lead and create a perception of confidence early in the match.

RELATING TO THE GROUP AND OTHERS FROM WITHIN AND OUTSIDE

A mentally efficient group is able to maintain quality interpersonal relationships with all members of the group – and, as a group, with others outside the group.

A mentally efficient group is able to maintain quality interpersonal relationships with all members of the group—and, as a group, with others outside the group. This is the case whether the group consists of two people—such as in doubles—or in the context of a school team, club, or association.

It is important for group members to be supportive of one another both on and off the court. In this respect, support involves helping one another strategically, technically, and emotionally.

The members of the group must also be able to come

together as a unit and relate to people who are not members of the group such as fans, the media, and other tennis teams.

GROUP REGARD

This dimension of the mentally efficient group has to do with the ability of the group members to consider themselves as unique individuals within the group and in terms of themselves. In this sense, the group regards each member as someone who exists over and above the group.

When the performance of the group does not equal its expectations—for instance when it loses a match they felt they should have won—the members of the group do not blame one another or particular members.

Rather, they regard themselves as an effectively functioning unit and an entity that is able to compete together as a team without loss of respect to individuals within.

They face each situation together and win or lose; they are able to maintain a high regard and respect for themselves both as a group effort, for one another, and as individuals making up that effort.

IMPROVEMENT AS A GROUP

A mentally efficient group values the process of their continuous improvement as a unit. The members of the group use feedback from their performance to develop action plans for their development that affects all members of the group on a continual basis.

Time is spent in determining the best strategies and procedures to achieve the most appropriate and effective performances. In doing so, doubles pairs and tennis teams are able to improve themselves as a group and decide on the most beneficial and effective actions to take in terms of ongoing improvement.

While tennis is considered primarily a sport played on an

The members of the group use feedback from their performance to develop action plans for their development that affects all members of the group on a continual basis.

individual or small group basis (doubles), mental efficiency is significant both as it relates to individual sports when they are played in the context of a team or club environment as well as team sports such as basketball or soccer.

As we have noted in this brief segment on group mental efficiency, the concept of mental efficiency is appropriate in both group and individual situations.

Moreover, group mental efficiency is similar to that of individual mental efficiency in terms of the qualities that are represented and many of the applications used to achieve its benefits to the fullest extent.

YOU CAN ATTAIN MENTAL EFFICIENCY

As you remain involved with the Mental Efficiency Program, you will witness for yourself the positive results.

Mental efficiency is not "something out there," nor is it a "quick fix" technique that you can plug in or purchase. It requires a program that depends on you. The program described in this book works and allows you to become a mentally efficient person in every aspect of your life.

Without hard work, nothing positive will result. This tried and true principle applies, of course, to your use of the Mental Efficiency Program.

So, as you remain involved with the program, you will witness for yourself the positive results. In this sense, you will be moving toward improved abilities and capabilities, along with enhanced quality of your tennis and your life.

Mental efficiency is the reward for the efforts you have put forth in implementing the Mental Efficiency Program as we have described it in this book.

Remember, when you are mentally efficient, you are in control of your thoughts, emotions, and physical actions. You learn to be absolutely effective with your time and efforts. You learn to set goals, to plan and progress, and to change when necessary to reach your goals and to be your best. You become an efficient user of time and energy.

The result is that you move in positive and worthwhile directions, both on and off the court, while enjoying the journey.

The road to achieving your best—as a tennis player and as a person—is more quickly and easily traveled when you are mentally efficient. Good luck!

AFTERWORD

The power of the individual is within. Use it wisely.
Nick Bollettieri

I have now been 37 years in the game of tennis at every level of play. The game has changed so much. My goal was simple. I wanted to provide junior players a place where they could become the best that they could be and not sacrifice their education in doing so. Looking back, I am selfishly proud of all that we have been able to accomplish.

It is no exaggeration to say that I have seen it all, experienced the best and the worst, and probably made every mistake in the book trying to accomplish what many believed I never would.

I didn't know that much about the game of tennis. I never played at the professional level. I didn't know about nutrition, physical fitness, sport psychology, sport science—these concepts didn't really exist in the world of sport when I began. I relied on my "street sense" and the belief that if you wanted something badly enough, and worked hard to get it, it would happen.

I also learned to surround myself with people who were smarter than me and to combine my gut instincts with their brains and skills. For me, that has paid off royally.

The Mental Efficiency Program shares the best of the Bollettieri experience and four decades of street savvy with the academics and knowledge of my friend Charles Maher, who without a doubt, ranks at the top of his field. Mental efficiency is both instinctual and learned. It combines the experience and expertise of a trained sport psychologist and a coach with the proven on-court technical capability.

It's not complicated, because that is not Bollettieri. It does work, because that is Bollettieri. And if it needs to change with times or with the game, we will do that because this is a dynamic program where you monitor and direct your own progress and track your own development. As your topspin serve improves, so does your ability to hit it under pressure time and time again. You grow physically and mentally in the same training program.

What you learn on the court you take into life. It's as simple as that. The Mental Efficiency Program provides you with the ability to perform at your best always—on and off the court, in and out of sport—and the tools to guide your own growth and development. It works for any sport, for any player, individual, or team, and helps you reach your goals easily and quickly by following the steps in the same way you would begin to learn the forehand stroke.

All my life, I have practiced mental efficiency, but it has taken me until now to get it down right on paper. That's where my staff and Charles Maher come in so strong. I have worked with some of the best sport psychologists in the business and experienced a wide variety of techniques to help enhance the learning process. Each is a little different and all have their merit and benefit. None, however, have the base of research or the programmed benefits that ours brings to each participant. Mental Efficiency works and reaches beyond the sport of tennis and benefits you in all areas of your growth and life.

I hope you will use this book often. It will help you reach your goals as it has helped me reach mine throughout all my life.

Nick Bollettieri
September 1994

REFERENCES

The research, professional, and technical references listed in this section are provided as empirical and technical support for the material presented in the chapters and for the Mental Efficiency Program. General references that overarch the entire book and program are listed first, followed by references for each chapter.

GENERAL REFERENCES

Bandura, H. (1986). *Social foundations of thought and action: A social cognitive theory.* Englewood Cliffs, NJ: Prentice-Hall.

Barlow, D.N., & Hersen, M. (1984). *Single care experimental designs: Strategies for studying behavior charge.* New York: Pergamon.

Bryan, A.J. (1987). Single subject designs for the evaluation of sport psychological interventions. *The Sport Psychologist, 1,* 283-292.

Butl, D. (1987). *Psychology of sport: The behavior, motivations, personality, and performance of athletes.* New York: Von Nostrand Reinhold.

Cox, R.H. (1990). *Sport psychology: Concepts and applications.* Dubuque, IA: William C. Brown.

Csikszehtmihalyhi, M. (1990). *Flow: The psychology of optimal experience.* New York: Harper & Row.

Donahue, J.A. Gillis, J.H., & King, K. (1980). Behavior modification in sport and physical education: A review. *Journal of Sport Psychology. 2,* 311-328.

Druckman, D., & Bjork, R.A. (Eds.). (1991). *In the mind's eye. Enhancing human performance.* Washington, DC: National Academy Press.

Druckman, D., & Swets, J.A. (Eds.). (1988). *Enhancing human perfor-*

mance: Issues, theories and techniques. Washington, DC: National Academy Press.

Elias, M.J. (1993). *Social decision making and lifeskills development: Guidelines for educators.* Gaithersburg, MD: Aspen.

Forman, S.G. (1992). *Coping skills interventions with children and adolescents.* San Francisco: Jossey-Bass.

Gallwey, W.T. (1974). *The inner game of tennis.* New York: Random House.

Locke, E.A., & Lathom, G.P. (1990). *A theory of goal setting and task performance.* Englewood Cliffs, NJ: Prentice Hall.

Maher, C.A. (1986). *Professional self-management.* Baltimore, MD: Brookes.

Maher, C.A., & Bennett, R.E. (1984). *Planning and evaluating special education services.* Englewood Cliffs, NJ: Prentice Hall.

Martens, R. (1991). *Coaches guide to sport psychology.* Champaign, IL: Human Kinetics Publishers.

Maslow, A. (1962). *Toward a psychology of being.* New York: Von Nostrand Reinhold.

Meichenbaum, D. (1977). *Cognitive behavior modification.* New York: Plenum Press.

Miller, G.A. Galanter, E.H., & Pribram, K. (1960). *Plans and the structure of human behavior.* New York: Holt.

Pervin, L. (1984). *Personality: Theory and research.* New York: Wiley.

Singer, R.N., Murphey, M. & Tennant, L.K. (Eds.). (1993). *Handbook of research on sport psychology.* New York: Macmillan.

Suinn, R.M. (Ed) (1980). *Psychology in sports: Methods and applications.* Minneapolis: Burgess.

Vander Avweele, Y., DeCuyper, B., Von Mele, V., & Rzewnicki, R. (1993). Elite performance and personality: From description and prediction to diagnosis and intervention. In R. N. Singer, M. Murphey, & L. K. Tennant (Eds.), *Handbook of research on sport psychology* (pp. 257-289). New York: Macmillan.

Von Bertalanffy, C. (1968). *General systems theory: Foundations, development and applications.* New York: G. Braziller

CHAPTER 1
Taking a Personal Perspective

Brustad, R.J. (1993). Youth in sports: Psychological considerations. In R.N. Singer, M. Murphey, & L.K. Tennant (Eds.). *Handbook of research on sports psychology.* New York: Macmillan.

Chi, M.T.H., & Rees, E.T. (1983). A learning framework for development. In M.T.H. Chi (Ed.), *Contributions in human development, Vol. 9* (pp. 71-107). Basel, Switzerland: Korgen.

Csikszehmihalyhi, M., & Rathunde, K. (1989). The psychology of wisdom: An evolutionary interpretation. In R.J. Sternberg (Ed.), *The Psychology of wisdom.* New York: Cambridge University Press.

Gendlin, E.T. (1981). *Focusing.* New York: Bantam.

Kobassa, S.C. Maddi, S.P., & Kahn, S. (1982). Hardiness and health: A prospective study. *Journal of Personality and Social Psychology, 42,* 168-177.

Singer, R.N. (1988). Psychological testing: What value to coaches and athletes. *International Journal of Sport Psychology, 19,* 87-106.

Smith, R.E. (1988). The logic and design of case study research. *The Sport Psychologist, 2,* 1-12.

Vealey, R.S. (1989). Sport personology: A paradigmatic and methodological analysis. *Journal of Sport and Exercise Psychology, 11,* 216-235.

CHAPTER 2
Becoming Aware of Yourself

Damon, W., & Hart, D. (1982). The development of self-understanding from infancy through adolescence. *Child Development, 53,* 831-857.

Diener, E. (1979). Deindividualization, self-awareness, and disinhibition. *Journal of Personality and Social Psychology, 37,* 1160-1171.

Glencross, D. (1993). Human skill: Ideas, concepts, and models. In R.N. Singer, M. Murphey, & L.K. Tennant (Eds.), *Handbook of research on sport psychology* (pp. 242-253). New York: Macmillan.

Johnson, D.W. (1981). *Reaching out: Interpersonal effectiveness and self-actualization (2nd ed).* Englewood Cliffs, NJ: Prentice Hall.

Martens, R. (1975). *Social psychology and physical activity.* New York: Harper & Row.

Mischel, W. (1986). *Introduction to personality*. New York: Holt, Rhinehart & Winston.

Nideffer, R.M. (1980). Attentional focus – Self-assessment. In R.M. Suinn (Ed.), *Psychology in sports: Methods and applications*. Minneapolis: Burgess.

Normon, D.A. (1976). *Memory and attention. An introduction to human information processing*. New York: John Wiley & Sons.

CHAPTER 3
Achieving Self-Motivation

Ackes, H.R., & Garske, J.P. (1982). *Psychological theories of motivation (2nd ed)*. Monterey, CA: Brooks/Cole.

Bandura, A., & Cervone, D. (1982). Self-evaluative and self-efficacy mechanisms governing the motivational effects of goal systems. *Journal of Personality and Social Psychology, 45*, 1017-1028.

Csikszentmihalyi, M., & Nakomura, J. (1989). The dynamics of intrinsic motivation. In R. Ames & C. Ames (Eds.), *Handbook of motivation theory and research. Vol 3* (pp. 45-71). New York: Academic Press.

deCharms, R. (1976). *Enhancing motivation*. New York: Irvington.

Deci, E.L., & Ryon, R.M. (1985). *Intrinsic motivation and self determination in human behavior*. New York. Plenum Press.

Eysenck, H. (1982). *Attention and arousal*. Berlin: Springer-Verlag.

Gould, D. (1983). Developing psychological skills in young athletes. In L. Wood (Ed.). *Coaching science update*. Ottawa, Ontario: Coaching Association of Canada.

Harter, S. (1978). Effectance motivation reconsidered: Towards a developmental model. *Human Development, 21*, 34-64.

Klint, K.A., & Weiss, M.R. (1987). Perceived competence and motives for participating in youth sports: A test of Harter's competence motivation theory. *Journal of Sport Psychology, 9*, 55-65.

Locke, E.A., & Latham, G.P. (1985). The application of goal setting in sports. *Journal of Sport Psychology, 7*, 205-222.

McClelland, D.C., Atkinson, J.W., Clark, R.W., & Lowell, E.L. (1953). *The achievement motive*. New York: Appleton-Century-Crofts.

Roberts, G.C. (1982). Achievement motivation in sports. In R. Teyung (Ed.), *Exercise and sports science reviews. Vol. 10*. Philadelphia: Franklin Institute Press.

Roberts, G. (1993). Motivation in sports: Understanding and enhancing the motivation and achievement of children. In R.N. Singer, M. Murphey, & L.K. Tennart (Eds.), *Handbook of research on sports psychology* (pp. 405-420). New York: Macmillan.

CHAPTER 4
Building and Maintaining Self-Confidence

Bandura, A. (1982). Self-efficacy mechanisms in human agency. *American Psychologist, 37,* 122-147.

Bandura, A. (1977). Self-efficacy: Toward a unifying theory of behavior change. *Psychological Review, 84,* 191-215.

Easterbrook, J.A. (1959). The effect of emotion on reevaluation and the organization of behavior. *Psychological Review, 66,* 183-201.

Fenz, W.D. (1975). Coping mechanisms and performance under stress. In D.M. Landers (Ed.), *Psychology of sport and motor behavior.* Penn State HPER Series No.10. University Park, PA: Pennsylvania State University Press.

Guyton, A.C. (1976). *Structure and function of the nervous system.* Philadelphia: Saunders.

Karterolistis, C., & Gill, D.L. (1987). Temporal changes in psychological and physiological components of state anxiety. *Journal of Sport Psychology, 9,* 261-274.

Sage, G.H. (1984). *Motor learning and control: Neuropsychological approach.* Dubuque, IA: Wm. C. Brown.

Selye, H. (1975). *Stress without distress.* New York: New American Library.

Vealy, R.S. (1986). Conceptualization of sports – Confidence and competitive orientation. Preliminary investigation and instrument development. *Journal of Physical Education, Recreation and Dance, 53*(3), 27-38.

Weinberg, R.S. (1985). Relationship between self-efficacy and cognitive strategies in enhancing endurance performance. *International Journal of Sport Psychology, 17,*135-155.

CHAPTER 5
Possessing Self-Discipline

Benson, H., Beory, J.F., & Carol, M.P. (1974). The relaxation response. *Psychiatry, 37,* 37-46.

Boutcher, S.H., & Rotella, R.J. (1987). A psychological skills education program for class & skill performance enhancement. *The Sport Psychologist, 1,* 127-137.

Crews, P.J. (1993). Self-regulation strategies in sport and exercise. In R.N. Singer, M. Murphey, & L.K. Tennant (Eds.), *Handbook of research on sport psychology* (pp. 537-563). New York: Macmillan.

Feltz, D.L., & Landers, D.M. (1983). The effects of mental practice on motor skills learning: A meta analysis. *Journal of Sport Psychology, 5,* 25-57.

Jacobson, E.J. (1938, 1976). *Progressive relaxation.* Chicago: University of Chicago Press.

Mahoney, M.J. Gabriel, T.J., & Perkins, T.S. (1987). Psychological skills and effective athletic performance. T*he Sport Psychologist, 1,* 181-199.

Noel, R.C. (1980). The effects of visual-motor behavior rehearsal on tennis performance. *Journal of Sport Psychology, 2,* 221-226.

Smith, D. (1987). Conditions that facilitate the development of sport imagery training. *The Sport Psychologist, 1,* 237-297.

Suinn, R.M. (1972). Removing emotional obstacles to learning and performance by visuo-motor behavior rehearsal. *Behavior Therapy, 31,* 308-310.

CHAPTER 6
Quality Interpersonal Relationships

Bennis, W., & Naus, B. (1985). *Leaders: The strategies for taking charge.* New York: Harper & Row.

Bredemeier, B.J. (1983). Athletic aggression: A moral concern. In J.H. Goldstein (Ed.), *Sports violence.* New York: Springer-Verlag.

Carron, A.V. (1982). Cohesiveness in sport groups: Interpretations and considerations. *Journal of Sport Psychology, 4,* 123-138.

Coakley, J. (1993). Socialization and sports. In R.N. Singer, M. Murphey, & L.K. Tennant (Eds.), *Handbook of research on sport psychology* (pp. 571-586). New York: Macmillan.

Gill, D.L. (1978). Cohesiveness and performance in sport groups. In R.S. Hutton (Ed.), *Exercise and sport science reviews, 5,* 131-155.

Johnson, D.W., Marvyoma, G., Johnson, R.T., Nelsen, D., & Skon, L. (1981). Effects of cooperative, competitive, and individualistic goal structures on achievement: A meta analysis. *Psychological Bulletin, 89,* 47-62.

Knapp, M.L. (1978). *Nonverbal/communication in human interaction (2nd ed.)*. New York: Holt, Rinehart, & Winston.

Lifebvre, L.M., Leith, L.L., & Bredemeier, B.B. (1980). Modes for aggression, assessment, and control. *International Journal of Sport Psychology, 11*, 11-21.

McKay, M., Davis, M., & Fanning, P. (1983). *Messages: The communication book*. Oakland, CA: New Harkinger.

Silver, J.M. IV. (1980). Assertive and aggressive behavior in sports. A definitional clarification. In C.H. Nadeau (Ed.), *Psychology of motor behavior and sport*. Champaign, IL: Human Kinetics Publishers.

CHAPTER 7
Developing Positive Self-Esteem

Brandon, N. (1983). *Honoring the self: The psychology of confidence and respect*. New York: Bantam.

Deci, E.L. (1980). *The psychology of self-determination*. Lexington, MA: Lexington Book.

Dweck, C.S. (1980). Learned helplessness in sport. In C.H. Nateau, W.R. Hollawell, K.M. Newell, & G.C. Roberts (Eds.), *Psychology of motor behavior and sport*. Champaign, IL: Human Kinetics Publishers.

Maltz, M. (1969). *Psychocybernetics*. Englewood Cliffs, NJ: Prentice-Hall.

Reyeski, W.L., & Brawley, L.R. (1983). Attribution theory in sport. Current status and new perspectives. *Journal of Sport Psychology, 5*, 77-99.

Wankel, L.M., & Kreisel, S.J.P. (1985). Factors underlying enjoyment of youth sports: Sport and age group comparisons. *Journal of Sport Psychology, 7*, 51-64.

Weiner, B. (1985). An attributional theory of achievement motivation and emotion. *Psychological Review, 92*, 548-573.

CHAPTER 8
Committing to Continuous Improvement

Callahan, E.J., & Ziegler, S.G. (1980). The application of within-subject design methodology to sports psychology. *Journal of Sport Behavior, 3*, 174-183.

Dorwick, P.W. (1991). *Practical guide to using videos in the behavioral sciences.* New York: Wiley.

Dorwick, P.W. (1983). Self-modeling. In P.W. Dorwick & S.J. Briggs (Eds.), *Using video: Psychological and social applications* (pp. 105-124). New York: Wiley.

Gross, R. (1982). (Ed.). *Invitation to life-long learning.* New York: Fowlett.

McCullogh, P. (1993). Modeling, learning, developmental, and social psychological considerations. In R.N. Singer, M. Murphey, & L.K. Tennant (Eds.), *Handbook of research on sport psychology* (pp. 106-126). New York: Macmillan.

Privette, G. (1983). Peak experience, peak performance, and flow: A comparative analysis of positive human experience. *Journal of Personality and Social Psychology, 83*(45), 1361-1368.

Seligman, M.P. (1975). *Helplessness: On depression, development and death.* San Francisco: Freeman.

Starker, J.L., & Deakin, J. (1984). Perception in sports: A cognitive approach to skilled performance. In W.F. Straub & J.M. Williams (Eds.), *Cognitive sports psychology* (pp. 115-128). Lansing, NY: Sport Success Associates.

Thomas, J.R., French, K.E., Thomas, K.T., & Gallagher, J.D. (1988). Children's knowledge development and sport performance. In F.L. Small, R.A. Magill, & M.J. Ash (Eds.), *Children in sports (3rd ed.)* (pp. 179-202). Champaign, IL: Human Kinetics.

CHAPTER 9
Taking the Mental Efficiency Advantage

Argyle, M., Furnham, A., & Graham, J.A. (1981) *Social situations.* Cambridge, U.K.: Cambridge University Press.

Carron, A.V. (1980). *Social psychology of sport.* Ithaca, NY: Movement.

Gill, D.L. (1984). Individual and group performance in sport. In J.M. Silver & R.S. Weinberg (Eds.), *Psychological foundations of sport* (pp. 315-328). Champaign, IL: Human Kinetics.

Hanrahan, S., & Gallois, C. (1993). Social interactions. In R.N. Singer, M. Murphey, & CK. Tennant (Eds.), *Handbook of research on sport psychology* (pp. 623-646). New York: Macmillan.

Zander, A. (1982). *Making groups effective.* San Francisco: Jossey-Bass.

APPENDIX

Summary Description of the Process of the Design, Implementation, and Evaluation of the Mental Efficiency Program

The following process occurred over the period of about 18 months, and it continues as this book goes to press. It rests on our professional experiences, research initiatives, and the support of the research cited in the References. We present a summary description of the process we used to design, implement, and evaluate the Mental Efficiency Program as a means of professional and technical documentation. We continue to develop and improve the Mental Efficiency Program at the NBTA and elsewhere, based on our research, program evaluations, and professional experiences.

1 We defined and described mental efficiency from a psychological perspective. In this regard, we considered mental efficiency as the ability of an individual (tennis player) to use his or her thoughts and emotions to be the best possible at what they do, whether this was on the tennis court, the classroom, in business, or elsewhere.

In particular, we found the concept of mental efficiency to be particularly appealing to us because efficiency has to do with the task of doing things without waste. An example of mental inefficiency is engaging in negative thoughts and emotions while someone is engaged in match play.

Further, the notion of mental efficiency was easily linked to the task of prevention of inefficiency or needless waste, that is, when you are mentally efficient, particular personal problems are prevented while positive benefits accrue to the individual.

Moreover, our experience in teaching tennis and other sports at the NBTA and in other settings indicated that mental efficiency was a positive state to aspire to by all athletes, indeed people from all walks of life. Relatedly, it was a term that we found to be useful and accepted by tennis players, coaches, and other athletes at the NBTA and throughout the world.

Finally, and most important, Bill Rompf was instrumental in helping us to define and describe what the program was about in terms of the notion of mental efficiency and related concepts.

2 As we began to design the Mental Efficiency Program for use at the NBTA and elsewhere, we decided that the program had to be something really valuable for a junior player, adult player, tennis coach, or the parent of a player. In this regard, through our prior professional experience, coupled with our research about program planning and evaluation, we identified ten criteria that needed to be met by the Mental Efficiency Program before we could "go public" with it. These criteria were the following:

1. NEEDS-BASED

The program had to address real human needs of individuals who play tennis. These included cognitive, affective, and psychomotor needs. That is, if particular needs were met, the individual who participated in the program would be a better player and person, given their natural talent, interests, and existing physical skills. In essence, the individual would be more mentally efficient as a tennis player and person.

2. DEVELOPMENTAL

The program had to incorporate principles and procedures from developmental psychology, cognitive psychology, and educational psychology in that the individual program participant (tennis player) would be considered as someone who has potential to continue to develop themselves, both on and off the court, in personally valuable ways. Hence, such developmental principles and procedures would be relevant and usefully applied as part of the program.

3. EDUCATIONAL

The program had to be organized so that each individual participant could educate themselves and be educated about how to be responsible for their own learning, performance, and development.

4. PREVENTIVE

The program had to allow each individual to learn how to prevent problems (mental and physical) from developing rather than reacting to and remediating problems after they have developed.

5. PRACTICAL

The program had to be able to be implemented at the NBTA and elsewhere in ways that were not disruptive to tennis instruction and related routines but that, indeed, complemented these routines, and therefore, could be considered as part of the instructional curriculum.

6. USEFUL

The program had to be perceived by individual participants as helping them attain important goals that contributed to effective tennis performance as well as to the quality of their lives.

7. SPACED REPETITION

The program had to rely on principles of learning that recommend that an individual (tennis player) acquires personal qualities and abilities—in this case those having to do with mental efficiency—by practicing skills (mental and physical) over time, such as during a semester at the NBTA, in spaced repetitive ways, rather than through massed practice.

8. MULTISENSORY

The program had to actively involve each individual participant in learning how to be mentally efficient as a tennis player and person. This multisensory approach meant that the program had to involve the person in visual learning experiences (e.g., reading, reviewing videotapes), listening (e.g., through group discussion, lectures, audiotapes), and through guided practice (e.g., imagery, physical application).

9. PROPER

The program has to use methods, procedures, and techniques that adhered to all legal strictures and ethical standards having to do with the instruction, education, and learning of individuals.

10. TECHNICALLY SOUND

The program had to be based not only on our own experience, but also on our research and evaluation activities, and in addition, relevant, basic, and applied empirical research in sport psychology, cognitive psychology, developmental psychology, educational psychology, and related areas of human performance.

3 We conducted thorough reviews of empirical research as it pertained to mental efficiency, mental skills training, counseling for performance enhancement, and personal development, among other areas. Although our particular emphasis, of course, was on tennis, we also reviewed relevant research from all other sports (team and individual). Our searches for research and evaluation articles and documents (both published and unpublished) relied on several kinds of

data bases and sources: PSYCLIT (Psychological Abstracts), SPORT (a.k.a.. SIRC), ERIC (Educational Resources Information Center), along with our own research and evaluation at the NBTA and elsewhere.

Our expectation was that the use of the range of data bases, to complement our own work, would reduce possible bias in designing the Mental Efficiency Program and widen our chances of identifying worthwhile methods for use as part of the program's design. Research and related references that we used to help design the program have been listed in the section before this one.

4 From the above three activities, we delineated and described seven personal qualities of mental efficiency that were to form the major dimensions of the Mental Efficiency Program. These seven personal qualities of mental efficiency and the associated abilities were considered and commented upon by panels of experts from psychology, education, tennis, and business in terms of conceptual clarity, meaning, and accuracy. Those seven personal qualities were:

◆ Personal Awareness

◆ Self-Motivation

◆ Self-Confidence

◆ Self-Discipline

◆ Quality Interpersonal Relationships

◆ Self-Esteem

◆ Continuous Improvement

5 Based on these personal qualities coupled with the range of research, evaluation, and professional experiences, we composed an initial program design document. This described the Mental Efficiency Program with respect to the following program design elements:

♦ Participant populations (e.g., junior, club, adult player)

♦ Cognitive, affective, and psychomotor needs of participants addressed by the program

♦ Program purpose and goals

♦ Program methods and procedures

♦ Sequence and timing of steps and activities

♦ Program personnel (e.g., qualifications, roles, and responsibilities)

♦ Program evaluation plan (who? how? what results?)

6 We then subjected the initial program design to reviews by NBTA tennis professional, students, and others, including thorough pilot testing activities at the NBTA.

7 We developed a revised and completed program design document that was implemented and evaluated at the NBTA. In this regard, our evaluations have primarily used idiographic (as opposed to nomothetic) research approaches where emphasis is on each individual as the unit of analysis and his/her own control. In particular, qualitative case methods and single subject research designs have been used. (For a detailed justification for this kind of approach to research and evaluation in sport psychology, you can refer to the article by Vander Avweele, De Cuyper, Van Mele, and Rzewnicki [1993] listed in the General Section of the References.)

8 We developed this book as a means of providing information about the Mental Efficiency Program to tennis players, their parents, and coaches. In this regard, the book is intended to be an educational product. As such, the book contains guidelines, methods, and procedures. However, the book should not be construed as a detailed curriculum guide or program implementation manual for installation of the

program at a tennis club or with a high school or collegiate team. If you are interested in how to implement the program for a number of participants, this information can be found in our *Curriculum Guide For Implementation and Evaluation of the Mental Efficiency Program* (call the NBTA at 813-755-1000; ask for the Mental Efficiency Department or the Pro Shop).

INDEX